Golf Digest's

COMPLETE BOOK OF

GOLF
BETTING
GAMES

Golf Digest's

COMPLETE BOOK OF

GOLF
BETTING
GAMES

RON KASPRISKE

AND THE EDITORS OF Golf Digest

DOUBLEDAY

NEW YORK   LONDON   TORONTO   SYDNEY   AUCKLAND

PUBLISHED BY DOUBLEDAY

Copyright © 2007 by Golf Digest Publications

All Rights Reserved

Published in the United States by Doubleday,
an imprint of The Doubleday Broadway Publishing Group,
a division of Random House, Inc., New York.
www.doubleday.com

DOUBLEDAY and the portrayal of an anchor with a dolphin
are registered trademarks of Random House, Inc.

Book design by Gretchen Achilles

Library of Congress Cataloging-in-Publication Data
Kaspriske, Ron.
Golf digest's complete book of golf betting games / by Ron Kaspriske
and the editors of Golf digest.—1st ed.
p. cm.
1. Golf—Betting. I. Golf digest. II. Title. III. Title: Complete
book of golf betting games.
GV979.B47K37 2007
796.352'6—dc22
2006039060

ISBN 978-0-385-51491-0

PRINTED IN THE UNITED STATES OF AMERICA

1 3 5 7 9 10 8 6 4 2

First Edition

CONTENTS

Over the last 20 years, thanks to being on the losing side of far too many wagers, I've paid for more vacations, daughters' braces, and drinks at the 19th hole than most of my golf buddies. But to me, it was worth it. Thanks Herb, Davey, Bulldog, Rudy, Wacker, Pittboss, Frazier, Oz, Brian, Simson, Wee Bob, Spou, Chris, Wally, Hugh, Doylee, Z, and Lumpy.

—Ron Kaspriske

FOREWORD
BY JERRY TARDE

I once wrote a book with Sam Snead called *Pigeons, Marks, Hustlers, and Other Golf Bettors You Can Beat.* As a result, I falsely became known as an expert on golf betting. Unlike Sam, I was a sandbagger without the game to back it up. It cost me any negotiating position I had on the first tee. Whatever wager I suggested was overly scrutinized, downgraded, and whittled into a losing proposition. If I offered to bet that a jack of spades would jump out of a sealed deck of playing cards and squirt cider in your ear, just as Damon Runyon said, I couldn't get a taker. And any thought of gaining a fair advantage in a $10 nassau, and I mean "fair advantage" in the best sense of the term, became a nonstarter when somebody in the foursome heard I wrote The Book. That other truism of Runyon's, "All of life is seven-to-five against," came true for me in golf.

The truth is, if Sam had any secrets, he didn't reveal them in my interrogations. We'd ride around the mountains of West Virginia in his pickup truck, getting gas at the fillin' station, catching trout in the pond outside his house, feeding the chickens on the farm, drinking iced tea hand-delivered by Mrs. Snead, day after day, but never dishing the real dirt on what he knew best—hustling rich guys with fast backswings for hundred-dollar matches.

At the end of those afternoons of interviews when I'd ask Sam about press bets and he'd tell me about his father, Harry, a big Dutch German with a bushy moustache who worked in the boiler room at The Homestead and served as captain of the hose-and-reel brigade of the Hot Springs Fire Department. He'd answer everything but what I'd asked, and we would slip over to the Lower Cascades course and play a little nassau. And Sam would hustle me just as surely as if he'd grabbed me by the ankles, turned me upside down, and shook every last quarter out of my pockets.

It was something to behold, Sam at work, and what secrets I've learned came only by observation and the accidental comment. The notes for the book weren't in the transcripts; they were in our matches.

He had an amazing ability to see what others missed. Sam could walk into a locker room and name every players' shoes by the way their individual gait had worn the leather. I'd say, "Art Wall." And Sam would say, "Funny feet. Very high instep with his toes turned up when he walks." This power of observation he applied to his matchmaking. "Pay close attention to their eyes," he let slip. "Fear shows up as an enlargement of the pupils."

Or he'd say, "Look at your opponent's lips on the first tee and keep checking. If a white rash shows around his mouth, he's probably got the heebie-jeebies—double the stakes." Look for a change in your opponent's putting style. . . . Watch for indecision on club selection. . . . Study the natural rhythm of his stride. If a fast walker suddenly slows down, or if a dawdler speeds up, it means he's on the ropes. Those were all Sam's tricks.

And then he had his caution flags: Beware of suntans darker than your own. Never bet a sick man. Stay away from the unemployed. Don't play a golfer who has a two-digit handicap and a 1-iron in his bag. Bet with strangers only after they've become friends.

His thoughts on match play were basic but profound. Play conservatively on the early holes. When in doubt, check your opponent's lie. After winning a hole, concentrate on hitting a solid drive. When the momentum is going against you, change the pace of the match. Never follow a bad shot with a dumb decision.

The secrets avoided direct inquiry. They spilled out sideways, walking to the next tee or over a Coke at the end—or simply from observing the master when he grabbed me by the ankles. Swing instruction came the same way. If you asked him how to hit a high hook, he'd take his 2-iron, make a graceful waggle, and launch the ball on a rising trajectory that curved left before disappearing into the clouds. "How'd you do that, Sam?" you'd ask. "Here, want to see it again?" he'd say.

Sam was golf's greatest bettor in my book. He didn't gamble for as much money as others. He certainly didn't brag about his winnings. There's no mention of it on his Hall-of-Fame plaque. But he played anybody anywhere for anything, and he did it relentlessly for all 89 years of his charmed life.

This book breathes the same passion for playing the game. Ron Kaspriske and the editors of *Golf Digest* teach you the lessons of golf betting in all its multifarious and intoxicating forms. They've assembled the most complete guide to betting games ever. And they've even found the secrets. I think Sam would have loved this book.

ACKNOWLEDGMENTS

I'd like to thank my fellow editors at *Golf Digest*, particularly Melissa Yow, Jerry Tarde, Matt Rudy, Guy Yocum, and Bob Carney, for their contributions to this book. I'd also like to thank sports psychologist Gio Valiente and handicap guru Dean Knuth for providing insight on golf and gambling.

Golf Digest's

COMPLETE BOOK OF

GOLF
BETTING
GAMES

KNOW THE RIGHT BET FOR YOU. Sun Tzu, a Chinese general who lived in the sixth century B.C., became famous for writing in his book *The Art of War* that most battles are won or lost before they are ever fought. The same holds true with wagers. Knowing your strengths and your opponent's weaknesses, and understanding what game is appropriate for the course you are playing and what amount to wager, is far more important than playing well once the game begins.

NEVER BET MORE MONEY THAN YOU ARE COMFORTABLE LOSING. Anytime a wager escalates to an amount higher than your comfort level, the tendency is to focus on the fear of losing the cash instead of on the shot you are about to hit.

FIND THE SQUIRM POINT OF YOUR OPPONENT. This complements the second commandment. There is an amount of money that the thought of losing is too much for your opponent to bear. That's the minimum amount you want to bet. There's a good chance your opponent will fold under the pressure of potentially losing that amount and never really focus on the golf game.

NEVER ACCEPT A BIG BET IF YOU DON'T KNOW THE GAME. It's like playing a golf course for the first time. Almost every golfer will tell you he or she would have played the course differently if given another chance. Well, it takes a couple of trial runs before the basic strategy of a gambling game becomes clear. Set the wager low until you get the hang of it.

WHEN CHOOSING A PARTNER, PICK THE BEST GOLFER AVAILABLE. It's always enticing to choose a high-handicapper because of the strokes that player will get in a match. But dealing with the pressure of a match almost always causes high-handicap players to play below their potential. Meanwhile, the best players are used to the tension and often thrive.

USE SIDE BETS AS INSURANCE. Side bets are a good way to double your winnings or protect yourself from a bad bet. If you're a good putter, suggest playing "snake," a three-putt game.

DON'T PUSH WHEN THINGS ARE GOING BAD. Vegas gamblers will tell you it takes more guts to walk away from the table after losing a walletful of cash than it does to sit there and try to win it back. If your side is getting its butt kicked, this is not a good time to double the bet by "pressing." Wait until your play improves. If it doesn't improve, take your beating and try again next week.

NEVER EASE UP. Your opponents might be your friends, and one of them might have an uncle in the hospital, but the minute you start backing off, you invite disaster. Either your opponents will take it as an obvious insult to their ability (perhaps damaging a friendship), or your big lead will vanish because they will thrive on the momentum of winning a couple of holes. Step on your opponent's throat and hold it on the ground until the match is over. Then you can be friends again.

PLAY YOUR HARDEST DOWN THE STRETCH. Whether a press is on the line, a side bet is still to be determined, or there's a chance to cut into a deficit, playing well over the final few holes on the front and back nines is much more important than playing well at the start of the match. Finish strong.

ALWAYS PAY OR COLLECT THE BET AT THE END OF THE ROUND. No excuses.

INTRODUCTION:
THE HISTORY
OF GOLF GAMBLING
AND THE USGA'S POLICY

Golf and gambling are so intertwined that it's hard for many to imagine playing the sport without having a bet on the line. Whether it's the $1 match billionaires Bill Gates and Warren Buffett play or the $400,000 that Vegas gambler Billy Walters claims to have earned for holing one putt, the allure of the wager is enticing for most golfers. It's an odd partnership since most golfers will agree that the sport is hard enough without the added pressure of putting money on the line to make hands shake and stomachs sink. Perhaps for the same reason that people ride triple-loop roller coasters, the danger, excitement, and tension of testing one's level of comfort is the reason golfers are willing to wager $50 when they have only $20 in their pocket.

Does golf need gambling in order to be interesting? Probably not. But in a poll that *Golf Digest* recently conducted on course gambling, only 7 percent of golfers said they never gambled when they played. That means roughly 5 million avid golfers in the United

States have played with a wager on the line. It's also worth noting from the poll that nearly two-thirds of golfers were capable of losing $25 or more in bets every time they teed it up, yet one in three said all it would take is a $5 bet for them to get nervous over a three-foot putt.

"I would guess of the 7 percent of golfers who said they don't gamble, a few might have been fibbing," says Gio Valiente, a sports psychologist who works with many golfers on the PGA Tour. "Gambling in and of itself is addicting. It puts people in a flow state, a situation where someone's attention is 100 percent engaged on that one thing. Golf can do that, too, but I think for a lot of golfers who play regularly, they need that extra adrenaline rush of having a wager on the line to keep their interest on the round undivided. It's like skiing on a slope that's harder than your skill level. You have to be completely focused on the mountain or you'll wipe out."

The games golfers play are as intricate and enticing as some of their names: skins, nassau, Hammer, Hawk, Lone Wolf, Three-Club Monte, and Snake. Skins and nassau, incidentally, are the most used of all golf gambling games. In a *Golf Digest* poll, 39 percent of all gambling golfers used skins as their standard game, and 32 percent used the nassau. According to the U.S. Golf Association, the game of skins gets its name from the word "syndicates." This term was in use for the skins-game format from at least 1950, and the USGA suggests "skins" was just an abbreviated way of saying it. The nassau, meanwhile, gets its name from Nassau Country Club on Long Island. John B. Coles Tappan, the club's captain in 1900, is said to have created the game (you play separate matches for the front nine, the back nine, and the overall 18) because he didn't like lopsided 18-hole matches. If you were getting killed on the front nine, you could still win the back and not be thrashed so thoroughly.

Equally as famous as the games golfers play are the golfers who made a reputation—and sometimes a living—by winning golf bets. Sam Snead, who won 82 PGA Tour events and seven major championships, was probably the most famous tour professional associated with gambling. In his book *Pigeons, Marks, Hustlers, and Other Golf Bettors You Can Beat*, Snead wrote that his game of preference was a $5 nassau, six ways. In other words, it's a match where the front nine is worth $5, the back nine is worth $10, and the overall 18 is worth fifteen bucks. But he played for real money, too—and sometimes whatever item of value he could get his hands on. Snead said he once won $10,000 in a week in Florida on what began as a $5 bet. He also played for, and won, a full set of tires. It wasn't the amount of money that piqued Snead's interest; it was the betting.

Perhaps the most infamous golf gambler and hustler of all time was Alvin Clarence (Titanic) Thompson, who died in 1974 at the age of 82. He was a legend in the first half of the 20th century for the wagers he made—and collected. Thompson was a hustler and would do things such as wager he could hit a golf ball 500 yards, then when someone agreed to the bet because it seemed impossible, Thompson would tee one up on a frozen lake. He also knew that applying Vaseline or axle grease to the face of a driver would greatly reduce the chance of hitting slices or hooks (almost every hustler knows this old trick). Thompson reportedly beat gangster Arnold Rothstein—the man behind the Black Sox scandal of the 1919 World Series—out of $30,000 in a golf match. He also won $3,000 in a match against Byron Nelson, shooting a 70 to Nelson's 68. Of course, the three strokes Thompson was given at the start of the match were just enough to win the bet.

Matches like that are few and far between, and the winners and losers don't necessarily want to gain publicity from their bets. Remember, good hustlers don't want to be known or they will never get another bet— so it's hard to separate fact from fiction when it comes to golf gambling stories handed down over the decades. There are many tall tales. Daredevil Evel Knievel claims to have paid a stiff price for losing a golf bet. Evel says that in a match at SeaCliff Country Club in Huntington Beach, California, he bet a known cheat that the loser of their match would either pay $7,000 to the other or have a finger cut off. Knievel lost the bet. "I'm a man true to my word," he says, "so I said, 'I'm not going to pay you; I'm going to cut off my finger instead. So I let the cart guy cut off a tip of my finger. I put it in my pocket and headed to a nearby hospital, and a doctor sewed it back on, and that was that."

So where and when did it all start? To no surprise, it was the Scots who made golf wagering what it is today. Betting is as much a part of life in the United Kingdom as is the comings and goings of the royal family, and wagering on golf dates back to the 1600s. The first known reference to handicapping in golf comes from the diary of a University of Edinburgh medical student. Thomas Kincaid wrote in 1687, "At golf, whether it is better to give a man two holes of three, laying equal strokes, or to lay three strokes to his one and play equal for so much every hole." According to Dean Knuth, *Golf Digest* professional adviser and creator of the USGA's handicapping system, Kincaid, like many of us on a Saturday morning, was trying to determine how to make a wager between two golfers equitable when their skill levels on the course weren't. According to Knuth, most clubs had a person assigned to the task of making golf wagers equitable. The Scots first called handicapping "assigning the odds."

"Golf in the old days, as in archery competitions before it, was a prelude to feasting," says Knuth. "Awards were handed out to the winners at the feasts. Archery and golf were secondary. In the early days of assigning the odds, a player would get one stroke every nine holes, or every six holes, or every three holes. I believe that medal score was the common way of playing, so a player got to take his strokes off his score at the end. If the players played match play, the player getting the stroke got to choose where he got it in the group of holes, because of stroke allocation. Handicapping the holes didn't exist yet.

The handicap system used today by the USGA was developed by Knuth in the early 1980s. A graduate of the United States Naval Academy, Knuth first created a course rating system and then was invited by the USGA in 1981 to be its director of handicapping. Within a year he devised the Slope Rating that courses across the nation use to determine how a player's handicap index applies to their track. Of course, handicaps are in use to make matches between players of different abilities more equitable, but this also makes golf wagering easier. This notion led the USGA to implement a "policy on gambling."

Although the USGA acknowledges that the presence of gambling can threaten the integrity of the sport, it makes it clear that wagering on a round of golf does not threaten the amateur status of a player. In other words, earning $20 in a nassau does not constitute becoming a professional—even if it happens on a daily basis. Furthermore, because gambling is so prevalent in the sport, the USGA claims it "does not object to informal wagering among individual golfers or teams of golfers when the players in general know each other, participation in the wagering is optional and is limited to the players, the sole source of all money won by the players is advanced by the players on themselves or their own teams and the amount of money involved is such that the primary purpose is the playing of the game for enjoyment."

The USGA cautions clubs by saying that it "is opposed to and urges its Member Clubs, all golf associations and all other sponsors of golf competitions to prohibit types of gambling such as: (1) calcuttas, (2) other auction pools, (3) pari-mutuels and (4) any other forms of gambling organized for general participation or permitting participants to bet on someone other than themselves or their teams."

Of course, even if the USGA did object to all forms of gambling, it's unlikely that most golfers would stop.

ALL SQUARE: Anytime in match play when opponents are tied.

ALTERNATE SHOT: A form of match play where partners play one ball and alternate who hits each stroke until the ball is holed. The partners also alternate who hits each tee shot no matter which player finished the previous hole.

AMBROSE: A type of scramble where each player's handicap is used to tabulate the team's overall score. Typically this is done by adding up the handicaps of each player on the team and dividing by the total number of teammates. The team would receive a stroke or strokes on the holes where the team handicap is applied. Sometimes the division of the total team handicap is double the normal amount. In other words, the handicap of a four-player team would be determined by adding each player's handicap together and dividing by eight instead of four.

AUTOMATIC PRESS: An additional mandatory bet that is activated at a certain time in a match. For instance, if a player goes two down on the front nine, then an automatic press might start for the remaining holes. If someone goes two down in the press bet, then a third bet starts. Press bets are typically concluded at the end of the front or back nine.

BEST BALL: A game format where any number of teammates play their own ball until it's holed, but only a certain number of their scores on each hole count for the team score. Best ball is sometimes known as "four ball."

CHOKING: See *Gagging*.

CLOSED OUT: When a golfer has an insurmountable lead in a match and the bet has already been decided.

CONCEDED (ALSO KNOWN AS GIMME): In match-play format, any player can concede, at any time, an opponent's next shot and deem it to be holed. This is usually done to save time.

DORMIE: When one side of a match can do no worse than tie, such as being three up with three holes to play.

EXTRA HOLES: A sudden-death tiebreaker in which the first player or team to have a lower score than their opponent wins the bet, match, etc.

FOUR BALL: See *Best Ball.*

GAGGING: The pressure of a wager forces opponents to play worse than their typical ability level—sometimes considerably worse.

GAMESMANSHIP: Any tactic—sportsmanlike or not, subtle or obvious—that is done to distract and possibly cause an opponent to make a mistake on the course. Some classic forms of gamesmanship include playing at a slower pace than normal to make your opponent get impatient; jingling change in your pocket while your opponent is getting ready to putt; and reminding your opponent before he or she tees off that there is a water hazard on the left side of the fairway.

GARBAGE: See *Junk.*

GETTING/GIVING SHOTS: The stroke adjustment a player or team receives or gives based on handicaps.

GIMME: See *Conceded.*

GROSS: A player's actual score without factoring in handicap strokes.

GUNCH (ALSO KNOWN AS JAIL): Thick rough, trees, a spot off the fairway where there's a lot of trouble.

HALVED: In match play, when two or more opponents tie for the low score on a hole.

HAM AND EGG: When one golfer is playing badly, the teammate plays well, and vice versa. This allows a team to stay competitive despite inconsistent individual play.

HONORS: The player who had the lowest score on the previous hole is said to have honors on the tee box. This means that they can play the first shot of the group. The order in which the golfers will play for the first hole is usually determined by lot.

INDEX: Short for *Handicap Index*. The official USGA rating a golfer is given based on the scores from the 10 best of their last 20 rounds. That figure is used to determine a player's handicap on each course.

JAIL: See *Gunch*.

JUNK: Any number of side bets that are being wagered in addition to a bigger bet. These side bets are typically achievement-related, such as hitting a green in regulation or getting up and down from a bunker for par or better.

LEAD HORSE OR HORSES: The player or players in a team match who are being counted on to lead the team to victory.

MARK: See *Pigeon*.

MATCH OF CARDS: A form of tie-breaking where players check their scores on specific holes to determine the winner of a bet, match, etc. Typically, the match of cards starts with the course's No. 1 handicap hole. The player or team with the lower score on that hole wins. If there is a tie between opponents, the match goes to the second hardest hole. Sometimes, the match starts at the 18th hole and goes backward.

MODIFIED STABLEFORD: A game in which points are awarded to each player depending on their score for that hole. Typical point distribution: one point for a bogey, two for a par, three or four for a birdie, and four or six or eight for an eagle. Sometimes, the game can be played with points being subtracted for high scores.

PENCIL-WHIPPED: Being outsmarted or out-negotiated when agreeing to a golf wager.

PIGEON (ALSO KNOWN AS A SUCKER OR MARK): Any person who accepts a bet with little or no chance of winning it.

PLAYING POSSUM: See *Sandbagging*.

PRESS: An additional bet made during a round. The press is a new bet, usually for the same amount of the original bet, which is conducted on the holes remaining to be played. It typically concludes when the front or back nine is completed.

PROGRESSIVE: A bet that doubles every time a certain achievement is made.

PROX (ALSO KNOWN AS PROXIES): The player's shot that is closest to the pin and on the green in regulation.

READY GOLF: An accepted time-saving method in which the player who is ready to hit the next shot can play, regardless of whether they are the farthest from the hole or have honors on the tee.

SANDBAGGING (ALSO KNOWN AS PLAYING POSSUM): Any form of deception that gives the impression that a golfer's ability on the course is inferior to what it really is. Then, at a crucial moment, the level of play improves and the player wins the bet.

SCRAMBLE: To save par from a difficult lie on the golf course; or a gambling format where teammates are allowed to choose the best of their shots on each hole to compile one team score.

SKIN: The monetary value of a particular hole. In a skins game, the low score (unmatched) on a hole is said to have won the skin. If the low score is tied, that monetary value carries over to the next hole, and now two skins are on the line.

STACKED IT (ALSO KNOWN AS STIFFED IT): Hitting a ball close to the hole.

STIFFED IT: See *Stacked It.*

SUCKER: See *Pigeon*.

THREE-JACKED: Three-putting a hole.

VANITY HANDICAP: When a player's handicap is lower than it should be in an effort to make the player appear to be better than his or her true ability.

YOU'RE AWAY: The player farthest from the hole is said to be "away" and can play the next shot.

CHAPTER I

GAMES FOR TWOSOMES

Whether it's a quick nine holes after work with the guy in the cubicle next to you or a match against your old nemesis, there are literally dozens of games you can play against a lone opponent. Even if paired with two strangers who fill out your foursome, most of these games can still be played without interrupting the rounds of the other two players.

AIR HAMMER

A skins game in which the value of a hole can be doubled, but only when a shot is in the air. So if there's a $1 bet on a hole, and a player's opponent hits a tee shot that's bound for a water hazard, while the shot is in the air the player can literally yell "Hammer!" at his opponent, and the bet has now doubled to $2 for that hole. Low score wins on each hole (unlike skins, the bet typically doesn't carry to the next hole when the previous hole is halved). Of course, the opponent has the right to "hammer" back when the player hits an errant shot, as long as it's airborne, so that $2 bet could go to $4 or $8, etc.

STRATEGY TIPS: Obviously you'll want to "air hammer" someone if their shot is heading for big trouble. But if you get hammered, don't fret. Your opponent still has to play the hole and can screw it up just as easily. If you are in big trouble, don't try for the miracle shot. Play safe and wait for your opponent to make a mistake.

BACKGAMMON (ALSO KNOWN AS HAMMER)

Holes are worth a predetermined amount—like a skins game—and the low score wins that hole. However, during the play of the hole, either player can double the bet, at anytime, if they think they can win the hole—even after the other player has holed out. The opponent can accept the new wager or decline it. An opponent who declines loses the original amount the hole was being played for. An opponent who accepts can double the new bet, and now it's up to the other player to accept or decline the new bet. This process can continue until both players hole out.

STRATEGY TIPS: A decisive advantage off the tee is grounds for doubling the bet. It's also wise to double if your opponent gets into a very difficult up-and-down situation near the green. If you're looking for a reason

Indigo

Store# 00287 Indigo Toronto Eaton Centre
220 Yonge Street
Toronto,ON M5B 2H1
Phone: (416) 591-3622
Fax: (416) 591-6791
* Thank you for shopping at Indigo *
Store# 00287 Term# 004 Trans# 195664
Jump Operator: 138CP   12/17/2007 20:26
GIFT RECEIPT
****
GOLF DIGESTS COMPLETE BK OF   CEJF
0385514913

****
A GIFT FOR YOU
****
Holiday returns accepted until
Jan 13 2008. Items returned
with a gift receipt and in store
bought condition may be exchanged
for a credit note for the value
of the item on the receipt.
Store# 00287 Term# 004 Trans# 195664
GST Registration # R897152666

0028700401956642

Si vous n'êtes pas entièrement satisfait d'un de vos achats, n'hésitez pas à le retourner pour un remboursement ou un échange dans un délai de 14 jours. Nous exigeons cependant que l'article soit dans le même état qu'au moment de l'achat et que vous présentiez un reçu provenant d'une de nos librairies. Les articles accompagnés d'un reçu-cadeau et retournés en condition de revente peuvent être échangés ou remboursés par une note de crédit pour la valeur de l'article lors de l'achat. Veuillez noter qu'aucun échange ou remboursement ne sera accepté pour les magazines ou les journaux.

If, for any reason, you purchase an item that is not totally satisfactory, please feel free to return it for refund or exchange within 14 days; we simply ask that the item be returned in store-bought condition and be accompanied by a proof of purchase from any of our stores. Items accompanied by a gift receipt and returned in store-bought condition may be exchanged or refunded onto a credit note for the value of the item at the time of purchase. Please note we cannot provide an exchange or refund of magazines or newspapers.

Si vous n'êtes pas entièrement satisfait d'un de vos achats, n'hésitez pas à le retourner pour un remboursement ou un échange dans un délai de 14 jours. Nous exigeons cependant que l'article soit dans le même état qu'au moment de l'achat et que vous présentiez un reçu provenant d'une de nos librairies. Les articles accompagnés d'un reçu-cadeau et retournés en condition de revente peuvent être échangés ou remboursés par une note de crédit pour la valeur de l'article lors de l'achat. Veuillez noter qu'aucun échange ou remboursement ne sera accepté pour les magazines ou les journaux.

If, for any reason, you purchase an item that is not totally satisfactory, please feel free to return it for refund or exchange within 14 days; we simply ask that the item be returned in store-bought condition and be to double the bet, a good time to do it is when your score is all but secured and your opponent has a tricky putt to win the hole. This extra pressure often produces a missed putt.

BACK IT UP

A variation on the traditional skins game. The player who wins a hole has the option of pocketing the value or leaving it on the table and doubling the value of the skins by winning the next hole—known as "backing it up." In other words, a player wins a skin worth $1. If this golfer leaves it on the table and wins the next skin, the value doubles and the player wins $4 for the two skins (two skins worth $2 each). If someone else wins the hole, that winner gets only the original value of two skins ($2). If the hole is halved (tied), the value is reduced to a normal skin amount for the next hole (now three skins for $3). Remember, the goal is to *back up* a win with another win. A variation of the game gives a double bonus for a back-it-up skin that is won with a natural birdie or better. In essence, those skins would be worth $8.

STRATEGY TIPS: After winning a skin, consider two things before trying to "back it up": how your opponent is playing and whether the next hole suits your eye. If you are using handicaps, always back it up if the next hole is a stroke hole for you. (A stroke hole is a hole in which you subtract a stroke from your score but your opponent doesn't.)

BAG RAID

See game description under **Pick-Up Sticks** in this chapter.

BOBBY JONES

A great stroke-play or match-play game for two players who have vastly different handicaps. Each player has to hit a tee shot and then play the other's tee shot the rest of the way into the hole. In order to make this fair, the high-handicap player should have the opportunity to choose between their own tee shot and the better player's tee shot to prevent the better player from deliberately hitting a poor shot. That means the player with the higher handicap always tees off second. The game can also be played with handicap strokes.

STRATEGY TIPS: Off the tee, the weaker player should play aggressively and try to hit the ball as far as possible—with one exception. If the better player hits a tee shot into the water or out-of-bounds, the weaker player should play conservatively off the tee and force the better player to try to make bogey or better by having to play their own tee shot.

BRIDGE

See game description in the Foursomes chapter.

CLOSEOUT

A match-play competition with a potential for two bets. If the first match ends before the 18th hole, then a second match begins for half the amount of the original wager, and it's played over the remaining holes.

STRATEGY TIPS: Getting waxed over 12–15 holes doesn't sting as much if you can win half your money back at the end. So if you're losing in a big way, try to hang on as long as you can so your opponent tires in time for the new bet to start. If you are getting strokes, pay particular attention if they come on holes late in the match, giving you a decisive advantage on the second bet.

CUBE

A nine-hole, match-play game in which the player with the shortest tee shot on the first hole owns the "cube."

The cube is an imaginary item that allows the owner to double the wager for the front nine—at any time—until the outcome is decided. Once the bet is doubled, the cube is transferred to the opponent, who now has the opportunity to double the bet. The transferring of the cube can continue several times until the nine-hole match is decided. On the 10th tee, a new cube is given to the shortest hitter and a new bet begins.

STRATEGY TIPS: The original bet for each nine should be low, since doubling can escalate if the match goes back and forth. The player who owns the cube controls the game, so taking a decided advantage in the match gives you a great opportunity to double your money. If you're three up with four holes to play, it's time to use the cube.

HAMMER

See game description under **Backgammon** in this chapter.

MATCH PLAY

Each player vies for the lowest score on each hole (their total number of strokes for the entire round is irrelevant), and one of them wins the match when they have won more holes than remain to be played. For instance, a player who wins the first hole is said to be one up. If the opponent wins the next hole, the match is "all square." If the opponent then wins the next hole, the opponent is one up and the player is one down. The game ends when someone has won more holes than there are holes remaining to be played. If the number of holes a player is up is equal to the number of holes remaining, the match is said to be "dormie," and the player who is leading can do no worse than tie. Handicap strokes are often applied in this game to make it equitable. If a player has a handicap of six on a course and the opponent has a handicap of 12, the inferior player would be able to subtract a stroke from his or her score on the six hardest holes on the course.

STRATEGY TIPS: Match-play veterans will tell you that no matter how big your lead is, never let up or go easy on an opponent. It's OK to play safe and force the player who is trailing to play aggressively—and possibly make mistakes—but don't play so safe that you start giving away holes. Each hole gives golfers a chance to start anew, so don't worry if you play one hole very poorly. Your stroke-play score is irrelevant.

MULLIGANS

See game description in the Foursomes chapter.

A match-play competition with three bets: one for the front nine holes, one for the back nine, and one for the entire eighteen. Each bet is typically for the same amount, so a $5 nassau is actually a $15 bet overall. During the match, a variation of the nassau allows for the player who is trailing to request a new bet (usually for the same amount as one of the legs of the nassau) for the hole or holes remaining on that nine. That player calls for a "press." For instance, if someone is two down with three holes to play on the front nine, that player can call for a press for the remaining three holes. That means there is a new three-hole bet. The other bet also remains intact. Sometimes the player in the lead can refuse a press, so it's good to clarify what form of nassau you'll be playing. Another variation allows for an automatic press when the deficit in the front- or back-nine match gets to a certain point, such as two down, by either player. Press bets can be pressed, so there can be several bets going on at the same time.

STRATEGY TIPS: If handicap strokes are being used and presses are allowed, it's good to press on holes where you are getting a stroke and your opponent is not. It's also a good idea to press on holes that suit your game or hurt your opponent, such as a long par 5 that you can reach in two but your short-hitting partner cannot. The final few holes on any side are crucial, so don't ease up, even with a big lead.

ONE CLUB

Competitors play an entire round with only one club. Match or stroke play can be used to determine the winner. This game can be modified to include a putter. Competitors have a choice of selecting which club each one will use, or a specific club can be agreed upon before the round begins.

STRATEGY TIPS: If you can pick, go with a 7-iron or 6-iron. These clubs have enough loft to hit shots around the green and just enough distance to make some par 4s reachable in two, and most par 5s reachable in three. If you're using an iron on the green, focus on not breaking the wrists at impact, as the loft on the club will make the ball skid. Try to putt with the leading edge. Off the tee, concentrate on keeping the ball in play and not trying to play the hole in a traditional sense. If there's a good spot to lay up on a hole, use it.

ONE ON ONE

A points game. Drives in the fairway longer than 150 yards earn one point, longer than 200 yards earn two points, longer than 225 yards earn three points, and longer than 250 yards earn four. (You can also have a six-point bonus for a 300-yard drive in the fairway.) Approach shots that hit the green (they don't have to be in regulation, but there can be a one-point bonus if one is) from 100 yards or less earn one point, longer than 100 earn two points, longer than 150 yards earn three points, and longer than 200 yards earn four points. Putts made from 30 feet or longer earn four points, from 15 to 30 feet earn two points, and from outside the length of the flagstick earn one point. The player with the most points wins and is paid the difference by the loser.

STRATEGY TIPS: Two-point achievements can easily be racked up in this game, with 200-yard drives in the fairway and 101-yard approach shots that hit the green, so focus on keeping the ball in play.

PICK-UP STICKS (ALSO KNOWN AS BAG RAID)

A match-play or nassau game with a twist: A player who wins a hole gets to remove a club from the opponent's golf bag. (Usually opponents agree that the putter is not eligible for removal.) Once a club is removed, it cannot be used again for the rest of the round.

STRATEGY TIPS: The driver would seem a good candidate as the first club to go, but this strategy could backfire as your opponent will likely hit more accurate tee shots with a shorter club. Go for the wedges first, particularly the sand and lob wedges. Or, take the fairway woods and hybrids out first to force your opponent to hit driver off as many tees as possible.

SECOND CHANCE

Each player plays two balls and records the best score on each hole in a nassau match against the other player. This game is great for a round on an empty course, or on one in which you have long waits between holes.

STRATEGY TIPS: The second ball is often the better ball, but consider playing conservatively with your first ball and being daring with the second. Otherwise you might end up with the same score for each ball.

SKINS

See game description in the Foursomes chapter.

STROKE PLAY

The player with the lowest score after a predetermined number of holes is the winner. Handicap strokes can be subtracted from the total score to make the competition more equitable. A single bet can be made, or the loser can pay a predetermined amount for every stroke more than the winner had.

STRATEGY TIPS: Making a big mistake on one hole can prove a lot more costly than bogeying your way around the golf course, so always look to avoid big trouble on any hole. Making a bogey on a par 3 by laying up in front of the green, chipping on, and two-putting might be hard on the ego, but it's a lot better than hitting a tee shot into the water, taking a drop, skulling the next shot into a bunker, and then three-putting for a quadruple bogey. It's probably better not to pay attention to what your opponent is doing on a hole. You could lose focus on your own game.

SUPER NASSAU

A match-play competition where there are nine or more potential bets over the course of the match. Every three holes, one bet ends and a new one begins for a total of six, three-hole bets. There also are three bigger bets in a traditional nassau format—the front nine, the back nine, and the overall 18 holes. The three big bets should be worth three times the amount of the smaller bets. So, say, $1 for the three-hole bets and $3 for the nine-hole and 18-hole bets. Players can also decide if there are presses for each bet.

STRATEGY TIPS: There is a lot of action going on, so try not to get sucked into whether you are up or down in all the matches. Instead, focus on your game. Let your opponent keep score. He will really be bogged down in the math while you focus on the hole. If you just lost a hole and a mini-match is still on the line, play conservatively on the next hole (rather than aggressively) and wait for your opponent to make a mistake. You never want to lose two holes in a row.

TEE TO GREEN

The longest shot off the tee in the fairway gets two points, and the longest shot that holds the green (from any spot on the course) gets one point if it wasn't in regulation and three if it was. Bonus points can be awarded for good drives and approach shots that are longer than a specified length. For instance, any drive that is measured at 250 yards or longer that's in the fairway gets an extra point. Any approach shot longer than 180 yards gets an extra point.

STRATEGY TIPS: Being the longest hitter doesn't mean you'll rack up points off the tee. Go for accuracy by selecting shorter clubs. If you are a short hitter, you have a chance for redemption by having longer shots into greens. So play to your strengths.

THREE-CLUB MONTE

Each player gets to choose three clubs from their bag and use them exclusively during the round. It should be determined before the round if the putter counts as one of the three or can be used in addition to the other clubs selected. Match play or stroke play can be used to determine the winner.

STRATEGY TIPS: A pitching wedge, 5-iron, and a good driving club is probably the best combination. If the putter counts as one of the clubs, you should add it to your three-club selection unless you are comfortable putting with a hybrid or 3-iron.

TROUBLE

See game description in the Foursomes chapter.

WORST BALL

Each golfer hits two tee shots, and then plays another two balls from the position of his or her worst ball. This continues until the worst ball after each shot is holed and the score is recorded. Of course, in putting that means holing two putts. The game can be played without the putting feature to speed up play.

STRATEGY TIPS: Focus on hitting shots you know you

can repeat with some consistency. So if a hybrid off the tee is more reliable than a driver, then dump the driver. Pars are rare in this game and birdies are even more unusual, so don't worry if you are making bogeys. Just avoid the really big scores.

YARDAGES

See game description in the Foursomes chapter.

CHAPTER 2

GAMES FOR THREESOMES

Every Saturday across the nation, you can bet that more than a few usual foursomes become threesomes when someone has to drop out. While that ruins the opportunity of playing many team wagers, there are still plenty of gambling games three golfers can play.

BACK IT UP

See game description in the Twosomes chapter.

BEVERAGE-CART BONUS

A traditional skins game in which the amount up for grabs doubles when the beverage cart appears on the hole the group is playing. There can be no intentional delay if you hear the cart approaching. It must arrive during the normal course of play. No beverage cart on the course? Double the bet when the ranger drives by.

STRATEGY TIPS: There's not much strategy to this game except for bearing down on holes that are worth double.

CHAIRMAN

A variation of the game Rabbit. The first player to win a hole becomes the "chairman." Each subsequent hole won by the chairman is worth a predetermined amount. If the chairman ties for the low score, this person does not win anything, but retains the chair. When the chairman does lose a hole outright, the chair passes to the player with the lowest score.

STRATEGY TIPS: Once you get the chair, don't take unnecessary risks to win holes. If you hit your tee shot out of bounds, you've pretty much assured yourself of losing the chair. Conversely, if you don't have the chair, go ahead and play aggressively in an effort to get it. If you hit a shot close, you'll put pressure on the player with the chair to take risks.

DOUBLE TROUBLE

In this stroke-play game, golfers try to avoid making the high score on two consecutive holes. If a player can't avoid it, he must pay a point for every shot higher he is than the other two players. For instance, if after having the high score on a hole, a player makes a 6 on the next hole compared to a 4 for one competitor and a 5 for the other, he must pay two points to the player with the 4 and one point to the player with the 5. If a player has the high score (unmatched) on one hole and ties for high score on the next, only the player who had a lower score must be paid. If the player ties or has the high score on three consecutive holes, the point values double: Making a 6 to another player's 4 means the higher score pays the lower score four points instead of two. If the player ties or has the high score on four consecutive holes, the point values triple. The point values can increase beyond that, but typically stop at triple their original value no matter how many holes after the fourth that a player has the high score. Handicaps can be used in this game.

STRATEGY TIPS: Essentially, you accrue points by staying out of big trouble in this game. But if you find yourself facing the prospect of having the high score on consecutive holes, do everything you can to minimize the damage. In other words, play hard and try to salvage a bogey or double bogey. If you are in the woods and know you're on your way to having the high score for the second consecutive hole, don't try to force the issue. Punch out, wedge on, and save a stroke or two. Then be sure to play conservatively on the next hole to avoid having to pay double points.

ENGLISH (ALSO KNOWN AS TRIPLES)

Six points are at stake on every hole, and the group decides how much each point is worth. Four points go to the player with the low score and two points to the player who has the second-lowest score. If two players tie for the low score, they split the six points. If all three players tie, each gets two points. If two players tie for the second-lowest score, they get a point apiece. The player who has earned the most points at the end of the round is paid by the other two players. That amount is determined by the difference in points accumulated. The player with the second-highest total also is paid by the player with the lowest point total.

STRATEGY TIPS: Your actual score for each hole doesn't matter as much as finishing a hole with a better score than your opponents', so pay attention to what they lie on each hole. Just don't let it distract you from the shot at hand. If both of your opponents hit wayward shots, consider playing safe on that hole to ensure a chance at picking up the four points. Handicaps can be used with this game.

HARD WORK

A skins-game format in which each hole has a value determined by its difficulty. Determine an amount for the easiest hole on the course—typically the 18th. The holes are ranked on the scorecard (although your group can rank holes in any manner). Once you've decided what the easiest hole is worth, the value of the other holes can be determined in inverse relation to that amount. In other words, the No. 1–handicap hole would be worth 18 times the amount of the easiest hole. The No. 2–handicap hole would be worth 17 times the amount of the easiest hole. The low scorer on any hole wins the value of that hole. The value of holes that are halved can either carry over and be added to the value of the next hole or be lost. Handicaps can be used with this game.

STRATEGY TIPS: Make sure the scorecard ranking of handicaps for holes matches what your group considers to be the correct degree of difficulty for each hole. For instance, a 210-yard par 3 might show up on the scorecard as the No. 11–handicap hole, but most players will tell you that a 210-yard par 3 is a lot harder to par than a 420-yard par 4, which might be the No. 4 handicap. If you go by the rankings on the scorecard, there could be a "big-money" hole or two that plays to your strengths, so study the card carefully before starting the round.

HAWK

A variation of the game Wolf. One golfer is designated as the "hawk" on each hole, and that designation rotates among the members of the group after each hole is completed. After all three players have teed off, the hawk either chooses one of the other two players as his partner in a one-hole, best-ball competition (with handicaps) or selects an imaginary partner who has already made net bogey on the hole. If the hawk wins the hole with his imaginary partner (it's a best-ball tournament), he earns two points. If the opponents win the hole, they get one point each. If the hawk chooses a partner from one of the other two players in the group and wins, they each get a point. If they lose, the player with the imaginary partner gets two points. A variation of this game allows for the hawk to play the hole alone, winning three points if he scores lower than the two real players and the one imaginary partner, in other words, a net par or better. If the hawk loses alone, the opponents each get a point and the hawk loses a point. No points are awarded on holes that are pushed.

STRATEGY TIPS: Pay attention to where each player in the group is getting a stroke. On a hole where no strokes are given, it's almost always to your benefit to pick the imaginary partner. The only time you should play alone is if the two opponents are in trouble off the tee and you are either getting a stroke on the hole or have hit a par-3 green in regulation.

INVISIBLE MAN

A skins-game competition where the value of a skin doubles if the lowest score (net) not only beats the other players in the group but also beats the invisible man's consistent score of par. So winning a hole with a net birdie, for instance, causes the value of the hole or holes won to double because the invisible man matches the pot. If the low score ties the invisible man, the player is still paid the normal value of the skin or skins. However, if a hole is won with a net bogey, the value of the hole or holes is cut in half since the invisible man takes a cut. This prevents anyone from winning a bunch of skins with a less-than-stellar performance on one hole.

STRATEGY TIPS: Make your opponents putt out when they have a chance to win a skin, even if it's a tap-in. You just never know. An opponent who misses will either halve the hole or likely earn only half of what could have been earned for those skins. Pay attention to what holes you are getting strokes on, and really focus on making a gross par by getting a tee shot in the fairway and getting the ball somewhere on the green or close enough that an up-and-down is realistic. A net birdie can really pay in this game.

LET IT RIDE

Players earn points for making bogey or better on each hole. A typical point distribution is 5 for a bogey, 15 for a par, 30 for a birdie, 60 for an eagle. After earning any points, the player has the option of banking them or "letting it ride," meaning the point total can still grow on subsequent holes. The point values usually double for every hole they aren't banked. However, if the points aren't banked and the player makes double bogey, the total goes back to zero. Banked points can't be taken away and will be credited to the player at the end of the round. The player with the highest point total is paid a predetermined amount for every point higher than those scored by the opponents. The player with the second-highest point total gets paid by the player with the fewest points.

STRATEGY TIPS: Bank birdies and eagles the minute you earn them since they are worth so much more than a bogey or par. Bogeys and pars are good let-it-ride candidates unless a particularly tough hole is coming up. But if you just made par and a short par 3 or easy par 5 is on the horizon, let it ride.

LONE WOLF

On each hole, a player is designated the "lone wolf" and tees off last. The title rotates so each player gets to be lone wolf six times during the round. After watching the first player tee off, the lone wolf can choose that player as a partner and play a best ball against the remaining player for that one hole, or pass on that person as a partner. After the second player tees off, the lone wolf can again choose the second player as a partner or pass up that opportunity and play that hole alone. If the lone wolf chooses a partner and wins the hole, the two of them each get a point. If the lone wolf plays the hole alone and wins, he gets two points. If the lone wolf plays with a partner and loses the hole, the opponent gets two points. If the lone wolf plays alone and loses, the two opponents get a point each. This game can be played in a foursome as well. A lone wolf who wins alone in the foursome game typically gets three points instead of two. A group that beats a lone wolf in the foursome game gets one point apiece.

STRATEGY TIPS: Pay attention to how you are playing that day. If you have confidence, play alone as the lone wolf as often as you can, especially if both players hit weak or mediocre tee shots. If the other two players hit good tee shots, select the second player. It's always good to play alone as the lone wolf on short par 3s when your opponents have missed the green off the tee. If you hit the green, at worst you will halve the hole.

ONE CLUB

See game description in the Twosomes chapter.

QUOTA

See game description in the Foursomes chapter.

RABBIT

The first player to win a hole is said to have the "rabbit" by the tail. The other two players in the group try to steal the rabbit by making a lower score than the player with the rabbit on ensuing holes. (Handicaps can be used.) If the player holding the rabbit wins the next hole, he or she has the rabbit by the leg. That means the two opponents have to free the leg before they can steal the rabbit (thus having to win a combined two holes). If the player with the rabbit wins a third hole, he or she now has both legs. That means the opponents would have to win three holes before stealing the rabbit from the player in possession. Halving a hole with the player in possession of the rabbit is useless. The winner of this game is the player in possession of the rabbit at the end of the front nine and back nine. Or points can be awarded for the number of holes a player holds the rabbit, or both.

STRATEGY TIPS: Once you've won the rabbit, you have to do everything in your power to win a leg or two. Late in a nine-hole match, having a rabbit and one or two legs almost assures you of winning the pot. If you're chasing the player who has the rabbit, put the pressure on by playing aggressively and forcing your opponent to play aggressively to keep you from stealing it. This could lead to big mistakes by the rabbit holder. Getting hold of the rabbit early could cause you to play conservatively down the stretch, a strategy that might backfire.

RABBIT RUN

A variation of Rabbit. The goal is to capture as many rabbits as you can since each one is worth a predetermined amount. A player who wins a hole with a low score and thus grabs the rabbit has to win a second hole before another player does in order to capture the rabbit. Once captured, the rabbit is taken out of play and a new rabbit is put on the run. If someone grabs the rabbit but can't capture it before another player wins a hole, then there are two rabbits running and the next player to win two holes outright captures them both. If both rabbits aren't captured, then three rabbits are running, and so on. Any rabbits that are grabbed but not captured at the end of a nine-hole stretch are released from the game.

STRATEGY TIPS: Make the rabbits really coveted by setting the value of each one higher than your typical skin in a skins game. Streaky players can make a lot of money if they can string together three or four pars in a row.

RED-TEE RALLY

A nine-hole game played at the end of a golf trip or marathon day of 36 to 54 holes. It uses the skins-game format where all the players in the group play each hole from the forward tees. (No handicap strokes are given.) The only catch is, each player must use driver to tee off—even on par 3s.

STRATEGY TIPS: Just because you have to use driver doesn't mean you have to swing for the fences and try to drive every par 4. Swing in control on tight holes, and bunt the ball off the tee on par 3s. It's the par 5s where having a good drive can pay off. You might end up hitting a short iron onto a green to make an easy birdie. You've always wondered what playing the forward tees would be like; now's your chance to find out.

RED, WHITE, AND BLUE

A stroke-play game (with handicaps). All par 3s are played from the red (forward) tees. All par 4s are played from the white (middle) tees. And all par 5s are played from the blue (back) tees. Red, White, and Blue can also be played as a skins game with all par 3s worth one point, all par 4s worth two points, and all par 5s worth three points.

STRATEGY TIPS: There's not much strategy to this game other than focusing on the par 5s if they are worth more points than the other holes. The reason for moving up on the tees is that it encourages more pars and birdies on the tougher holes.

SKINS

See game description in the Foursomes chapter.

STROKE PLAY

See game description in the Twosomes chapter.

THREE BALL

Three nassaus or straight 18-hole matches are going on simultaneously between three players. Player A plays a match against Player B and another match against Player C. Player B plays a match against Player C in addition to the match with Player A. And so on.

STRATEGY TIPS: You might need to let a math whiz do the scoring. In fact, it's good to give the scoring duties to another player since you'll want to focus on your game. Remember, in a typical nassau, your opponent's play might dictate how you play a hole. For instance, if your opponent hits it out-of-bounds, you might play a hole conservatively and win it with a bogey. In Three Ball, with two matches going on, it becomes distracting to focus on your opponents' situations, so focus on your own game. If you're playing well, it will typically distract the other players from their own games. Don't play any more aggressively or conservatively than you usually do.

THREE-CLUB MONTE

See game description in the Twosomes chapter.

THREESOMES

Using the match-play format, one golfer plays against a team of two golfers, with each side playing one ball. The two-player team alternates shots or, if they are much higher in handicap than the single player, plays best ball. Handicaps should be used for this game unless all the players are similar in ability.

STRATEGY TIPS: If it's alternate shot, the single golfer has an advantage unless the twosome has two better players. If it's best ball, the twosome has a huge advantage unless the single player is a far better player. If it's your choice whether to play alone or with a partner, remember those two things.

TRIPLES

See game description under **English** in this chapter.

WOLF (ALSO KNOWN AS WOLFMAN OR HOG)

A threesome tees off. The player with the second-longest drive becomes the "wolf," and the other two golfers become "hunters." On par 3s, the player with the second-closest shot to the pin is the "wolf." Using handicaps, the wolf takes his net score for that hole, doubles it, and matches that combined score against the net scores of the opponents. If the wolf has a lower combined net score, then he wins a point from each of the two hunters. If the hunters have a better combined score, the wolf must pay each hunter a point. If the wolf and hunters tie, the bet can be either carried over to the next hole or lost. Honor on each tee box should rotate among the three players.

STRATEGY TIPS: The wolf has a huge advantage on par 3s if he is on the green because it's likely the worst score will be two pars. In a game with mid- to high-handicappers, you want to focus on having the second-longest drive on par 5s. The reason? Though you might not shoot the lowest score on the hole, the odds are long that the two hunters will play a par 5 in par or better. More shots are needed to par the hole, so there is more margin for error.

YARDAGES

See game description in the Foursomes chapter.

CHAPTER 3

GAMES FOR FOURSOMES

Most golfers will agree that the best gambling games involve a foursome. There's such an ebb and flow to golf, that when one member of the group is up, there's surely another who is down. Having a partner in a sport based on individual achievement makes the task seem less daunting, which is why most gambling games are designed around groups of four.

ACEY-DEUCEY

The player (or players) with the lowest score on each hole gets paid a predetermined amount by the player (or players) with the highest score. For instance, the four players in the group make 4, 5, 6, and 7 on the first hole. The player with the 4 gets $1 from the player with the 7. If two players tie for the lowest score, the player with the highest score has to pay each low player. In the example here, that amount could be $1 each or 50 cents, depending on what the group decides before the round. If two or more players tie for high score, they each pay the low player. (Again, it can be a division of a predetermined amount, or each can pay the entire amount.) Try to make the predetermined amount for low score easily divisible if you choose to divide the payment among the players with the high.

STRATEGY TIPS: If you hit a bad tee shot, it's more important to recover and play for bogey than it is to try to steal the low score for the hole. In other words, do everything you can to avoid ever making the high score. There's a huge advantage to teeing off last on the par 3s.

ALTERNATE SHOT
(ALSO KNOWN AS FOURSOMES)

Using a match-play or nassau format, two-player teams hit their tee shots and play each other's next shot, continuing to switch until one of the two balls is holed. That score counts as the team's score and is compared with the score of their opponents.

STRATEGY TIPS: Many people believe opposites attract, so a long hitter should be paired with a short hitter. But Tom Watson and Jackie Burke have each been quoted as saying that it's better to select a partner who has similar strengths and weaknesses. That way, the comfort level is increased. The twosome will typically be required to play shots from spots on the course they are used to seeing and hitting in a normal round. Comfort is key.

AMIGO

See game description under **Las Vegas** in this chapter.

AUTO WIN

In addition to winning a hole using a normal skins-game format, players can win holes automatically, regardless of score, by chipping in from anywhere off the green (including the fringe), holing out from a bunker, hitting a tee shot on a par 3 within the length of the flagstick (and making par or better), or by any number of achievements the group chooses before the round starts. That way, no player is out of the running for a skin or skins as a result of just hitting a tee shot out of bounds.

STRATEGY TIPS: Don't give up until the hole is finished. Play aggressively. If you can't win a hole with a low score, try to win it by chipping in, etc.

BEST BALL (ALSO KNOWN AS FOUR BALL)

Using the match-play format, teammates each play their own ball until it is holed, then they record the lower of the two scores as the team score. This score is matched against the team score of the other two players. Note: Best ball could also be played in a stroke-play format, with a total score for the 18 holes tallied and compared.

STRATEGY TIPS: If a player has already made an acceptable score on a hole or is in good shape to secure an acceptable score (par is usually acceptable), the partner can attempt a riskier shot and try to hole out for eagle or birdie. If a player is in trouble off the tee, the teammate should play conservatively, focusing on making no worse than bogey.

BEST BALL STABLEFORD
(ALSO KNOWN AS FOUR BALL STABLEFORD)

Two-player teams compete to rack up as many points as possible, using a best-ball format where only the team's low ball counts. This game can be played with or without handicap shots. A bogey is worth one point, a par two points, a birdie three points, and an eagle four points. Of course, the point allocation can vary depending on a preround agreement. The winners are paid for every point they have more than their opponents.

STRATEGY TIPS: If your partner is in a good position to earn points, that's your green light to take chances. Try to hole out for the big score. Conversely, play safe when your partner is in trouble, so your team doesn't get shut out on that hole. Your goal should be to earn at least one point on every hole.

BIG STICK

A stroke-play or match-play game in which the only rule is that all players have to hit driver on every tee box. (Par 3s can be excluded.)

STRATEGY TIPS: A great game for learning how to use your driver to hit shots various distances, with different trajectories and shot shapes (fades, draws, etc.). Don't just whale away. You'll be surprised at how much control you can gain with this club if you use it all the time. If you're a straight-ball hitter, this game can be easy to win.

BINGO BANGO BONGO

Points are achieved three different ways: (1) The first player on each hole to hit the fairway off the tee gets a point. (2) The first player on each hole to hold a shot on the green gets a point. (3) The first player to hole out gets a point. Each point is worth a certain value, and the points are tallied at the end of the round to determine the winners. The other players pay the person with the most points at the end of the round. And the person with the second-most is paid by the other two players, and so on. Obviously, the game has to be played in correct order (low score on the previous hole tees off first, and the farthest from the hole off the tee hits first), so you cannot play "ready golf." Keep pace of play in mind.

STRATEGY TIPS: Using driver off the tee isn't wise since a fairway wood or iron will probably put you in the fairway first. Also, you'll likely be the first to hit on the green since you are farther back than the players who used driver. A putt that comes up short of the hole is worthless, so hit your putts at a pace that puts the ball two or three feet past the cup. Focus on precise targets as part of your preshot routine, and your accuracy should improve.

BISQUE

Instead of the scorecard mandating where a player is given a handicap stroke or two, players are allowed to allocate their handicap strokes any way they wish during the round until they use up their allotted number of strokes. The only catch is that the strokes must be declared before the player starts a hole. Low net score wins and is paid a set amount by the other players, or the winner is paid an amount determined by the number of strokes she finishes lower than each opponent.

STRATEGY TIPS: Know your trouble holes before you play, and try to save your handicap strokes for these situations. Knowing that you get a stroke on a hard hole will help your score, and it will put you at ease so that you might play the hole better than usual. On a really tough hole, don't be afraid to use two handicap strokes (or more) if you have a really high handicap. Also, know what holes you typically would be getting a stroke on and determine if you need one to play that hole. If you can play a hard hole conservatively and make a respectable bogey, you might be able to save your strokes for an easy hole where a net birdie or eagle would give you a good chance of pulling away from the group.

BISQUE PAR COMPETITION

Each player in the group puts money into a pot and plays an 18-hole match against an invisible player who makes par (or bogey) on every hole. The object is to win holes by making a gross or net birdie or better. Players can allocate their handicap strokes any way they wish during the round until they use up their allotted strokes. The object is to have the best match-play score against the invisible player of anyone in the group.

Winning a hole makes a player 1 up, etc., just like in a standard match. Your individual score on each hole in relation to the other players in the group is irrelevant.

STRATEGY TIPS: Save as many handicap strokes as you can for the closing holes. Consider not using strokes early on if you halve a hole with the invisible player. You don't want to get more than 2 or 3 down at any point. Pay attention to where the difficult holes are and try to save a stroke or two for those holes. Use two strokes on a hole only if it allows you to win a hole or stay in the match.

BRIDGE

A stroke-play game in which each hole is worth a predetermined amount. Handicaps can be used. On the tee, a team of two players makes a bid on the maximum number of combined strokes (net or gross depending on what the teams decide) it will take them to finish the hole. For instance, the team decides it can play the hole in no more than 11 strokes. The other team has three options: Take the bet; take the bet and double it; or bid lower than the other team. If the other team bids lower than the team making the original bet, the first team has the same three options. The team with the lower score on a hole gets to make the first bid on the next hole.

STRATEGY TIPS: Start the bid a shot or two higher

than you think it will take you and your opponent to finish the hole. At best, your opponents will accept the bet and double it. At worst, they will counter with a predicted score that might be too hard to achieve. Then you can double their bet and make money by trapping them.

CHAPMAN SYSTEM
(ALSO KNOWN AS PINEHURST)

All four players tee off, and then teammates play each other's tee ball. Each team then selects one of its second shots as its ball and plays an alternate-shot format until the ball is holed and a team score is recorded. The player whose second shot was not selected by the team gets to play the third shot, and then it alternates between partners until the ball is holed. This can be played as stroke play or match play. Combining the two players' handicaps and dividing them by two can form team handicaps.

STRATEGY TIPS: When selecting the second shot, consider who is going to be hitting the third shot. If it's a par 5 and both second shots are in the fairway, consider choosing the weaker player's second shot, allowing the better player to hit the third onto the green. If both players are off the green on a par 4, the same holds true. In other words, if the second shots are similar, always allow the better player to play the third shot.

CHICAGO

Each player in the group starts with negative points, based on their course handicap, and then tries to get back to zero or better by earning points based on their play on each hole. Typically, a scratch golfer begins at minus-39, a 1-handicap starts at minus-38, and so on. Scoring usually is one point for a bogey, two for a par, four for a birdie, eight for an eagle. The player with the most points is paid the value of each point more than the other players scored. For instance, a player who gets back to zero is paid the amount of points finished ahead of the other players in the group. The other two players in the group pay the second-best finisher, and so on. To speed up play, those who can make no better than double bogey on a hole, and thus receive no points, can be deemed to have holed out.

STRATEGY TIPS: A high-handicap player who gets off to a good start by making more points than normal can focus down the stretch on keeping the ball in play and making pars or bogeys instead of taking chances. Better players have to attack par 5s, settling for no less than birdie or par in order to make up for the deficit they start the game with. Don't let a bad hole or two discourage you. A couple of pars or one birdie can make up for lost chances. Also, pay attention to how your score compares to the other scores. Don't take chances if you have the lead late in the round. Put the pressure on your opponents.

CUBE

See game description in the Twosomes chapter.

DAYTONA

Similar in style to Las Vegas. Two-player teams play a stroke-play format, each person playing his or her own ball. The two scores are combined to make one big score: The teammate with the lower score on a hole creates the first digit and the one with the higher score makes the second digit. So teammates with a 4 and a 6 on one hole have a combined score of 46. However, if both players make bogey or worse on a hole, the combined score should be the highest score possible. On a par 5, a double bogey and a bogey would create the one-hole score of 76. If a double-digit score is made, that figure is added. So a bogey and a 10 on a par 5 would be 610 points. The idea is to have the lowest point total at the end. The group with the higher score pays an amount for every point they finish ahead of the winning group.

STRATEGY TIPS: This game can be played with handicaps, but even if it isn't, playing safe is a lot better than taking a big number on a hole, so make sure you and your partner play within your limitations. The benefit of making a birdie on a hole does not compare with the pain of making a couple of double bogeys. And if you are hitting five off the tee on a par 5, you had better play hard. Earning a 10 or higher will break the bank, and your partner might not speak to you again.

DEFENDER

One member of a foursome is a hole's "defender," and that role rotates so everyone in the foursome gets to have the designation at least four times during the round. The defender's job is to get the lowest score on that hole; the other members of the group try to beat the defender. When the defender wins the hole, she gets three points (the amount a point earns is determined before play begins). A defender who ties for the low score gains 1.5 points and the other three players lose a half point. If the defender loses a hole, he or she loses three points and the other players gain a point. There are many variations to the point distribution. Another popular option is three points for winning a hole outright as a defender, two points for tying for the low score as a defender, and one point each for the other three players in the group if one of them beats the defender on a hole.

STRATEGY TIPS: The defender typically gets to tee off last, so play aggressively if other members in the group are in good position to score, and play conservatively when other members of the group are in trouble off the tee.

DOUBLE TROUBLE

See game description in the Threesomes chapter.

FAVORITE HOLE (ALSO KNOWN AS JOKER STABLEFORD)

Uses the Modified Stableford system (one point for a bogey, two for a par, four for a birdie, and six for an eagle). Before the round starts, each player selects the hole (or holes; you can select as many as the group wants) they think will be their best. Points earned by that player on that hole are doubled. The other players pay the player with the highest point total an amount for every point more than they scored. The player with the second-highest point total is paid by the other two players, and so on. A variation of the game allows for each hole to be selected by only one player. Each player selects four holes (two of the 18 holes are left unselected), but the selection process is handled like a draft. Determine the draft order by lot. To make it fair, reverse the draft order in the second and fourth rounds.

STRATEGY TIPS: Par 5s are typically the best choice for the favorite hole or holes since they are easy to par and there's a good chance at making a birdie or eagle on that hole.

FOUR BALL

See game description under **Best Ball** in this chapter.

FOUR BALL STABLEFORD

See game description under **Best Ball Stableford** in this chapter.

FOURSOMES

See game description under **Alternate Shot** in this chapter.

GREENSOMES

An alternate-shot, match-play, or nassau format between two-player teams. Both sets of teammates tee off. The partners then choose one of the tee balls to use for the rest of the hole. Typically, the person whose drive is not chosen for the team gets to hit the next shot.

STRATEGY TIPS: When choosing a partner, it's a good idea to find someone with a similar playing style. Otherwise you might find yourself hitting shots from areas on the course you aren't familiar with. In other words, a long-ball hitter might struggle if paired with a short hitter. Play your own game. Don't get caught up in trying to do too much to help your team. If you don't normally go for the green in two, don't do it here. Play the shots you are comfortable playing, and keep the ball in play. If both tee shots are in play, always choose the one that allows the better or more consistent player to hit the next shot. By doing so, you'll increase your odds of winning the hole since the better player should get the ball closer to, if not in, the cup.

GRUESOMES (ALSO KNOWN AS YELLOWSOMES)

A variation of Greensomes. It's an alternate-shot, match-play, or nassau formatted game. Each member of a two-person team tees off, and the opposing team gets to decide which tee ball the original team has to play for its next shot. The teams then play an alternate-shot format until the ball is holed. The person whose tee shot isn't chosen plays the second shot.

STRATEGY TIPS: When deciding which tee ball to

choose, consider which shot is in worse shape and who is hitting the second shot. When the tee shots are similar, always take the better player's tee ball—you want the weaker player to be hitting the important second shot.

HARD WORK

See game description in the Threesomes chapter.

HATE 'EM

Each player gets to choose three holes on the course (usually a par 5, par 4, and par 3) before the round starts. These are the holes that the player hates the most. These holes are played just like normal, but for betting purposes they count as pars to be tallied with strokes each player makes on the other 15 holes. The low score wins the bet. This can be played as a side-bet game or the main game, and it can be played with any number of golfers. It's better when played on a course all the players know.

STRATEGY TIPS: If you play a particular hole poorly every time, this game is for you. However, consider taking par on the three hardest holes on the course rather than on the ones you normally play poorly. This will give you incentive to play those nemesis holes better and take the pressure off you to score on the really hard holes.

HIGH-LOW

A two-player, stroke-play team game where a point is awarded to the team with the lowest individual score on a hole and a point is taken away from the team that has the highest individual score on a hole. If there are ties on either the high or the low, no points are won or lost for that part of the bet. A variation: A point is awarded on each hole to the lower of the two lowest scores from each group and the lower of the two highest scores from each group. In other words, one team makes a 4 and a 5 on a par 4. The other team makes a 5 and a 6. The one team's score of 4 is matched with the other team's score of 5, and the one team's second low score of 5 is matched with the other team's second low score of 6. In this case, the first team members would each win a point for the low and the high. This game can be played with or without handicaps.

STRATEGY TIPS: Having a consistent partner helps. Focus on avoiding big numbers and playing safe unless there is low risk in playing aggressively on any given hole.

HOG

See game description under **Wolf** in the Threesomes chapter.

IRONS ONLY

No woods or hybrids are allowed in this game, but players can have up to 14 irons in their bag. The format can be stroke play with the four players competing, or a best-ball match with teams of two competing against each other.

STRATEGY TIPS: Since the woods and hybrids are out of the bag, replace them with the longest irons you have and also add another wedge or two. It might be better to play long par 4s as three-shot holes rather than try to reach the green with two long irons that are harder to control.

JOKER STABLEFORD

See game description under **Favorite Hole** in this chapter.

KNOW YOUR LIMITATIONS

Before playing a hole, each player in the group has to predict the maximum score she will make on that hole, and points are awarded or taken away depending on what the player actually makes. Handicaps can be used, but for mid- to low-handicappers the game is often better without extra strokes. Scoring is as follows: If a player is brave enough to predict an eagle and makes it, he receives 12 points. If the player predicts a birdie and is successful, 6 points are awarded. For a successful par, 3 points are awarded. For a successful bogey, 1 point is awarded. For every stroke a player's actual score is above the predicted score, he loses that number of points. So making a bogey when a par was predicted means the player subtracts 1 point from his total point accumulation. Note: A player can predict a double bogey but doesn't earn any points for a successful prediction. However, points are lost for making a triple bogey or worse. If you score better than your predicted score, you earn only the points you would have earned if you had predicted correctly. The other players pay the player with the most points at the end of the round. The person with the second-highest number of points is paid by the two other players, and so on.

STRATEGY TIPS: This game is kind of like *Name That Tune*. You really need to know your game well. If you have played the course often, your predictions should fall in line with your typical scores. If you are using handicap strokes, predicting a net par or net birdie is a good bet on a stroke hole. If you are playing without strokes, making a birdie prediction on a short par 5 or drivable par 4 is not a bad bet. Remember, if you predict a birdie and make a par, you lose only 1 point, but if you are successful, 6 points is a nice haul for one hole. Don't be afraid to make bold predictions.

LAS VEGAS (ALSO KNOWN AS AMIGO)

Two-person teams play for a combined double-digit score on each hole. So if one player makes a 4 and his teammate makes a 6, their score for the hole is 46. (The lower number goes first.) The team score represents the number of points each team earns per hole. A team with an individual score in double figures puts that number first, so a 5 and a 10 would equal 105. Points are tracked throughout the round, and the differential is how the bet is paid. The team that made 46 would be paid 11 points by a team that made 57 on the same hole. Points can be worth any amount and teammates can rotate on each hole, but keeping track of the points can be more confusing this way. A variation: If one team makes a birdie, it can flip the opponents' score. Say the team with 46 included one birdie. They can change the other team's 57 to 75. The game can be played with handicaps.

STRATEGY TIPS: This is a game where going low really pays off. Focus on making birdies and pars. The high score rarely makes a difference unless the other team makes birdie, so don't worry if your team makes a par and a quadruple bogey. That score is still better than two bogeys. In other words, on a par 4, making a 4 and a 7 (47) is better than making a 5 and a 5 (55).

LEFT/RIGHT, NEAR/FAR

A two-player match-play game where one point is awarded on each hole for both the low individual score and the lowest team score. Partners are decided on each hole by tee shots. The players with the two tee shots farthest to the left are partners, and the players with the two tee shots farthest to the right are partners. Or, partners can be determined by pairing the players with the two shortest tee shots and the two longest. Generally, the teeing order rotates after every hole.

STRATEGY TIPS: The partnership that is comprised of the two right tee balls or the two short tee balls usually is at a big disadvantage. Typically these players either slice their tee shots or are considerably farther back in the fairway. So teeing up last in this game gives you an advantage. You can see the position of the other three balls and choose your partner with an accurate tee shot.

LET IT RIDE

See game description in the Threesomes chapter.

LONE WOLF

See game description in the Threesomes chapter.

MATCH PLAY

See game description in the Twosomes chapter.

MIX AND MATCH
(ALSO KNOWN AS RANSOM)

Two-player teams compete in three separate six-hole matches using a different format for each one. Typically the matches are best ball (net), alternate-shot (gross or net), and total score for both players (net). To figure the net score in alternate shot for a team, average the two handicaps together (round up), and that's the team's handicap for that six-hole stretch. Then check to see if that team has a stroke hole during that stretch. The amount of the bet for each six-hole match should be the same, and presses, like a nassau, are possible.

STRATEGY TIPS: All three games require a different strategy, so be prepared to switch your playing style from one hole to the next. Alternate shot is the most dramatically different. In alternate shot your main goal is to keep the ball in play. Don't leave your partner in big trouble. In best ball you can play more aggressively. Like all complex betting games, let your opponents keep score so you can concentrate on your game and not worry about the math.

MULLIGANS
(ALSO KNOWN AS NO ALIBIS)

A great stroke-play game for a group of high-handicappers. Each player's course handicap represents the number of shots they can replay as mulligans at any time or anywhere on the course without penalty. This game can't be used in conjunction with an official handicap round, but it's a great way for beginners to relax and learn from their mistakes. The lowest 18-hole score is compared against the other players' scores to determine how much is owed. Typically each stroke represents an amount of money each player has to pay. The two worst players pay the second-best golfer, and the player with highest score pays the third-best finisher.

STRATEGY TIPS: Be frugal with your mulligans. Use one only when you are reasonably certain that replaying a shot will save you a stroke or more on a hole or will guarantee a par or birdie. Putting is a great time to use a mulligan since making a four-footer or avoiding a three-putt is the fastest way to save shots.

NINE POINT

On each hole, the player in the foursome with the lowest score wins five points, the player with the second-lowest score wins three points, the player with the third-lowest score wins one point, and the worst score gets zero points. If two players tie for a specific score, they share the points. So if two players tie for the lowest score, each gets four points (five points, plus three points, divided by two). But the worst score or scores always get zero points.

STRATEGY TIPS: You never want to get shut out on a hole. Play conservatively unless you have a good chance at winning a hole with aggressive play.

NO ALIBIS

See game description under **Mulligans** in this chapter.

ODDS AND EVENS

Same game as alternate shot except one teammate tees off on all the even-numbered holes and the other tees off on the odd-numbered holes. After teeing off, the players alternate hitting the ball until it's holed.

STRATEGY TIPS: Forget the course's ranking of the 18 holes. If you look at each hole individually, you can determine whether the odd- or even-numbered holes are easier. Obviously, the weaker player should tee off on the easier group of holes. For instance, if three of the four par 5s on the course are odd-numbered holes, have the weaker player tee off on the odd-numbered holes. That way the team can recover from a bad tee shot and still make par or birdie on a par 5.

ONE CLUB

See game description in the Twosomes chapter.

PIG

Holes are worth different point values depending on your score. The point values escalate, and the winner is the player with the most points. For instance, on holes 1 through 6, a net eagle is worth 30 points, a net birdie is worth 20 points, and a net par is worth 10. Those point values escalate on holes 7 through 12 to, say, 45, 30, and 15, and increase again to 60, 40, and 20 on holes 13 through 18. At any point during the first six holes, a player can freeze the points he has earned. If that player doesn't freeze them, he runs a risk of losing them with a net double bogey or worse (better groups can change this to net bogey) before that six-hole stretch ends. Once points are frozen, no more can be earned for that set of six holes. One variation of the game forces a player to pay a penalty if he finishes the game with zero points. Another variation allows a player to unfreeze his point total with a net par or net birdie on an ensuing hole.

STRATEGY TIPS: Anytime a net eagle is made, freeze the points you have for that set of six holes. If you see you have a run of holes coming up where you are getting strokes, feel free to keep your point total unfrozen. But if you have to play a series of holes with no strokes, freeze the minute you make two pars or better. It pays to know where you are getting strokes.

PINEHURST

See game description under **Chapman System** in this chapter.

POINTS GAME (ALSO KNOWN AS UMBRELLA)

Two-player teams first determine the value of a point and then start the game at level one with a possible six points up for grabs on each hole. Two points are awarded to the team with the low ball, two points are awarded to the team with the low total, one point to the team with the ball closest to the pin in regulation, and one point to the team that makes a birdie. Handicaps can be used. On each successive hole, the team that trails in points can roll the level up one notch. If they do, points earned on ensuing holes become worth twice what they were at the start of the nine-hole match. Rolling can continue on every hole up to the tenth. Then the point value goes back down to level one. If a team wins all six points on a hole, they are said to have "poofed" the other team or covered them with an "umbrella," and the points are doubled. So, assuming the level has been rolled on each hole, poofing the other team on the ninth hole would be worth 108 points (six points × level nine × two for doubling = 108 points).

STRATEGY TIPS: Increase the level only if you feel your team has momentum or has an advantage on the next hole. If you're getting killed, keep the level low and it will be difficult to get beaten up monetarily, even if you don't recover. If you're ahead, encourage your opponents to raise the level, as this is the only way to win big money in the points game. Since low total is worth two points, it's important that neither partner take a big number on any hole. Play conservatively if you're not hitting it well or are playing a particularly tough hole.

POKER

Using the scores, each player tries to build the best five-hole poker hand possible on the front nine, and then the best five-hole poker hand possible on the back nine. Lower numbers trump higher numbers, so a player who makes four 3s on the front nine beats a player who makes four 4s. The hierarchy of poker hands is as follows: five of a kind, four of a kind, a full house (for instance, three threes and two fours), five-card straights (for instance, a 3, 4, 5, 6, and 7 on the scorecard), three of a kind, and two pair. Handicaps can be used, but the game is better without them. The player with the best hand on each nine wins an amount each player throws into a pot. A bonus can be given to a five of a kind.

STRATEGY TIPS: Since you can throw out your four worst scores on a particular nine, don't worry about playing safe. Be aggressive and try to make four or five pars.

QUOTA

Each player takes their course handicap, subtracts it from 36, and that becomes the point quota they have to make during the round. A bogey earns a player one point, a par two points, a birdie four points, and an eagle six or eight points. (Point allocations can vary and should be agreed upon before the round.) The player who earns the most points above the quota wins. If no one finishes above the quota, the player closest to the quota wins. The winner can be awarded a set pot or an amount for every point scored above the quota in relation to the other players. For instance, a player who made five more points than the quota would be paid the amount of three points by a player who made two points above their own quota and six points by a player who made one point less than their own quota. The payout system can penalize players who finish below their quota. In this example, the player with minus-1 would have to pay double for not reaching the quota.

STRATEGY TIPS: Try not to get shut out on any hole, even if that means playing conservatively on a dangerous par 3 by laying up. For a 15-handicapper, earning 21 points to reach a quota will take 15 bogeys and three pars. Naturally, making a birdie or eagle frees most players to play more aggressively.

RANSOM

See game description under **Mix and Match** in this chapter.

RED-TEE RALLY

See game description in the Threesomes chapter.

ROUND ROBIN

See game description under **Sixes** in this chapter.

SECOND BALL

A variation of best ball. If two players on opposing teams tie for the low score, then you revert to the scores made by their respective partners and the low player from the second ball wins the hole. If the second players also tie, the hole is halved. The game can be played as a nassau or a regular 18-hole match. Handicaps and presses also can be used.

STRATEGY TIPS: If you're the higher-handicap player on your team, play safe and try to avoid big numbers. That way, if the second-ball rule is in effect, your par or bogey ought to have a chance of winning the hole for the team. If you're the better player on your team, remember that holes are rarely halved in this game. Consider playing aggressively when your high-handicap player is in trouble. You probably are going to have to win the hole or your team will lose.

SIXES (ALSO KNOWN AS ROUND ROBIN)

Each player gets a teammate from the foursome for six holes. Then the teammates switch after each set of six holes, ensuring that everyone has a turn with another player in the group. The format for the bet can switch for each six-hole match or stay the same, but typically the format has to fit with match play. Some possibilities for the six-hole matches include best ball, low total, and alternate shot. Team skins can be used but should be employed as the format for all 18 holes. Handicaps can be used for this game.

STRATEGY TIPS: It's luck of the draw as to who your partner is and how well he or she is playing. What you can control is your own play, so focus on not making big mistakes and allowing your partner, when the lower-handicap player, to take risks. Taking the pressure off is the best way to help your partner play better.

SIXES NASSAU

Using the best-ball format, three nassaus are conducted during the 18-hole round, with each player in the foursome switching partners every six holes. Each six-hole match is a mini-nassau, with the first three holes counting as the front nine, the second three holes counting as the back, and the full six holes counting as the overall bet.

STRATEGY TIPS: Winning holes early in each match is crucial. It's the easiest way to win the "front three" as well as the overall six and secure two of the three bets per mini-nassau. If you get two up, consider playing conservatively the rest of the six-hole stretch and force your opponents to make aggressive plays to get back in the match.

SKINS

Each hole is given a certain value and the low score on that hole wins the amount, known as the "skin." If two players tie for the low score, the skin and its monetary value are added to the value of the next hole, and then two skins are up for grabs. This escalation continues until a player wins a hole. Since the value of holes typically increases as the game progresses toward the 18th, the winner is the player with the most money, not the most skins. Handicaps should be used with this game.

STRATEGY TIPS: Pay close attention to what your opponents lie. Play aggressively when things are tight and conservatively when you have a good chance of winning a hole with a bogey or par. Another strategy is to play aggressively early in the round when hole values aren't worth as much, and make up ground later in the round when the big-money holes are on the line. If you are using handicaps, it's good to play safe on stroke holes and try to turn a bogey into a net par and steal a hole. On the green, lag putts don't amount to much, so don't leave putts short.

STRIKE THREE

At the end of the round, each player throws out their three highest scores, and the lowest 15-hole score wins the pot or a point for each stroke lower he is than the rest of the group.

STRATEGY TIPS: Knowing you can throw out holes makes playing par 5s much easier because you can be aggressive and go for the green in two. If you've already made three double bogeys, it's wise to play safe the rest of the round.

STRING

See game description in the Multiple Groups chapter.

THREE-CLUB MONTE

See game description in the Twosomes chapter.

TRI-FOR-FREE

A game to consider if there's no time to warm up before a round. The first three holes of each nine aren't taken into consideration, so the game begins on the fourth hole of each nine. A point is awarded for the first player in the fairway and for the first player on the green. Two points are given for the low score for the final six holes of each nine (tie goes to the player who holes out first). The player with the most points wins and is paid by the other players the difference from their own point totals. The player with the second-highest point total is paid by the players who scored even less, and so on.

STRATEGY TIPS: Use the first three holes to get your swing and putting stroke grooved. Then focus on hitting fairways and playing to the fat part of greens with your approach shots, as this is the easiest way to rack up points. Since the game has to be played in correct order from farthest away from the cup, don't play slow.

TROUBLE

Players are saddled with points for a number of common mistakes during a round. The player with the fewest points at the end wins. This can also be played as a side-bet game. A typical point distribution is as follows: hitting a ball into the water or into a bunker (one point); hitting a ball out of bounds (two points); failing to get a ball out of a bunker in one swing (one point); three-putting (one point); four-putting (three points); whiffing on a shot (four points); failing to get a tee shot past the forward tee (one point), etc. Points can also be subtracted for making a birdie, holing out from off the green, or one-putting from outside the length of a flagstick.

STRATEGY TIPS: The great thing about Trouble is that, by playing safe for most of the round, you'll find that you've shot one of your best scores ever. Course management, particularly with high-handicappers, is often overlooked, but it has to be factored into the playing of this game. Getting saddled with a point here and there is no big deal. The key is to avoid the multiple-point penalties, so pay close attention to out-of-bounds stakes, and high rough where it's possible to swing and miss a ball.

TWO-PLAYER NO SCOTCH

A match-play game where two teammates tee off, then switch balls, playing each other's second shot. After selecting one of the second shots, the teammates play only that ball the rest of the hole, using a scramble format. That score becomes the team's score for the hole. The teams can also play this game as a nassau and the bets are set accordingly.

STRATEGY TIPS: Getting both tee shots in play is the most important factor, so players should not try hitting risky tee shots when an iron into the fairway will give them a good chance at making par or better once the scramble portion of the game begins.

TWO-PLAYER SCRAMBLE

A variation of the four-player game (see **Scramble** in the Multiple Groups chapter). Two teammates tee off and select one of the shots (usually the one in better position to record a lower score) as the one they will use. The two players then each hit another shot from this position, and again select one of those shots as the one they will use. This process continues until one ball is holed and a team score is recorded. Note: Once a shot is selected, the two players mark the spot where the ball came to rest and can drop within one club-length, no closer to the hole, to play their next shot. If the ball is at rest in a hazard, it cannot be dropped outside the hazard. If the term "ambrose" (see vocabulary) is used in conjunction with the scramble, a combined handicap of the two players is factored into the team score. For example, a player with a course handicap of 5 is paired with a player who has an 11 course handicap. Their team handicap would be the average—8. The lowest stroke-play team score wins this bet. The payout either can be a set amount or can fluctuate depending on the number of shots lower the winning team finished.

STRATEGY TIPS: The better player usually should be the second player to hit because it takes some pressure off the weaker player.

UMBRELLA

See game description under **Points Game** in this chapter.

A variation of the skins game. Each hole has a value based on the yardage of the hole. For example, if the group decides a yard is equivalent to a penny, then a 400-yard par 4 is worth $4. Holes are won when one player in the group has a lower score than anyone else. If two players tie for the low score, that amount can be carried over to the ensuing hole or holes. This game can also be played where hole values do not carry over. At the end of the round, each player adds up their cash earned and is paid or pays the difference between this amount and what the other competitors earned.

STRATEGY TIPS: Focus on the par 5s and try to keep the ball in play on those holes rather than hitting driver wildly or going for the green in two. A par has a decent shot at winning a par 5 in a group with mid- to high-handicappers since the margin for error is increased because it requires more good shots to play the hole well. In a group of good golfers, playing aggressively is more important than worrying about the score.

YELLOWSOMES

See game description under **Gruesomes** in this chapter.

CHAPTER 4

GAMES FOR MULTIPLE GROUPS

Whether it's for a big fund-raising tournament or a group of golfers who get together every Tuesday evening, assigning a gambling game for multiple groups is easy when you consider the skill level of the players involved as well as the personality of the competitors. Some games are more lighthearted than others, and some require a skill set some golfers do not possess.

1-2-3 BEST BALL
(ALSO KNOWN AS IRISH FOUR-BALL)

Each member of a foursome plays its own ball throughout the round. On the first hole, the lowest score of the group counts as the team score. On the second hole, the two lowest scores count. On the third hole, the three lowest scores count. On the fourth hole, it goes back to the lowest score counting as the team score. At the end of the round, all the scores used are tallied and compared with the combined scores of another foursome or foursomes. Note: This game can be played by groups of threesomes.

STRATEGY TIPS: Groups should play aggressively only on holes where the single lowest score counts. On a hole where three scores are needed, conservative play is prudent. Three bogeys are the least acceptable score.

14 CLUBS

Using the scramble format and the USGA limit for the number of clubs one player can carry, a foursome is given 14 clubs total (two players get four clubs, and two get three) with no sharing between players. The sets can consist of any combination of club—every player can have a driver, or wedge, or a putter if they wish.

STRATEGY TIPS: Every player should carry a putter, a tee club, and a high-lofted iron. The players with the four-club allotment (make them your better players) should consider including a wedge and/or a middle- to long-iron. Get creative with your shot selection, and just about any club in the bag can work for any shot.

AGGREGATE STABLEFORD

Teams (usually consisting of two or four players) try to amass as many points as possible, using a Modified

Stableford format for scoring (one point for a bogey, two for a par, three for a birdie, and four for an eagle). Handicaps are typically factored. The points each player on the team earns on each hole are combined with the scores of teammates for an aggregate total on each hole. The team with the most points wins.

STRATEGY TIPS: Before the round, assess which holes are easy and which holes will be difficult for all the groups involved, and try to predict what a good aggregate score will be on each hole compared to what other groups might score. Use your prediction chart to determine how each player in your group should play the hole. For a tough par 4, maybe a two-player team would be happy with three points. So if one player is in good shape to make par, the other player should play conservatively and try to make bogey or better. If one player makes birdie, the partner can play aggressively and try to exceed expectations for that hole.

BEST BALL

Although typically played as a match between members of a foursome, a best-ball tournament can be played as a stroke-play event among as many teams as desired. Each member of a team (twosome, threesome, foursome, etc.) plays his own ball throughout the round. The lowest score of any team member for each hole is recorded as a team score and matched against team scores from other groups.

STRATEGY TIPS: If your partner is on the verge of recording an acceptable score (or has already done so), play aggressively since you have nothing to lose. If your partner or partners are in trouble, play conservatively to ensure a decent score.

BLIND NINE

Competitors can use any 18-hole game format (a scramble is the most common), but after the round is completed, nine holes are drawn from a hat (or similar random selection) and thrown out. The remaining nine holes are used to tabulate the team score and are compared against the score of other teams. A foursome, using the stroke-play format, can play this game.

STRATEGY TIPS: Play hard on every hole, and don't be discouraged by playing one or two holes very poorly. There's a chance those holes could be thrown out of your team score. This game keeps golfers of varying abilities interested since they have the potential for amnesty on holes where they didn't make par.

CALCUTTA

A type of auction-pool wagering that can be applied to teams or individuals. Golfers bid, auction-style, on the golfer or team they think will win the tournament. All the money raised through the auction is combined. At the end of the tournament, the person or group who bid on the winning team wins a large percentage of the pot, if not all of it. Sometimes the bidders who picked the top three teams win money. It's OK to bid on yourself or your team in a calcutta.

STRATEGY TIPS: A golfer capable of playing far better than the handicap index often wins a calcutta involving handicaps. So selecting, say, a 15-handicap capable of shooting an 83 is better than selecting a 6-handicap who shoots roughly 77–80 every time he tees it up. In gross play, select a veteran team or player whose game is suited for that course.

CALLAWAY SYSTEM

Used for an outing where the majority of players don't have official USGA Handicap Indexes. The USGA stopped endorsing this method in the late 1990s, but it's still in use. Players can deduct a certain number of holes from their total score based on what they shoot.

For instance, players shooting 73 or lower deduct zero holes. Players shooting 106 or worse deduct their four worst holes. The higher the score, the more holes deducted. A variation of the game calls for the final two holes to count for all players. Check the Internet for a chart to see how many holes get deducted depending on a player's score.

STRATEGY TIPS: The steady player, who has one or two "blow-up holes" but otherwise plays fairly steady golf, has the best chance of winning this format, so focus on avoiding big numbers. If bogey golf is your game, don't take chances that could lead to big mistakes.

CHA-CHA-CHA

A stroke-play event with handicaps. The lowest score in a four-player group counts as the team score on par 3s. The two lowest scores on a par 4 count as the team score, and the three lowest scores on a par 5 count as the team score. Add up all those scores, and the team with the lowest score wins. Handicaps can be used in this format.

STRATEGY TIPS: Risk-taking on par 5s is not advisable, since all it takes is two bad scores on that hole to really screw up the team score. On the par 3s, however, fire for the flags.

CRISS-CROSS

Using the stroke-play format, a single player or any combination of players is assigned to a team. Once the 18-hole round is complete, the player or team is allowed to take the lower score of two holes that are paired together. Nine pairs of holes will be determined after the round at random or by an impartial committee. Each player or team then counts the lower score of each pairing as part of a nine-hole, stroke-play score. One suggested scoring method takes the lower score from holes 1 and 10, and from holes 2 and 11, etc. Most Criss-Cross tournaments use this pairing formula.

STRATEGY TIPS: Pay close attention to where you played poorly on the front nine because you might be able to make up for it with a good score on the corresponding hole on the back nine. If you have already recorded a good score on a front-nine hole, such as a birdie on a par 5, then it's OK to take chances and go for an eagle on the corresponding hole on the back.

DAYTONA

See game description in the Foursomes chapter.

The game is similar to a traditional scramble format, where members of a four-player team each get to hit a tee shot and only one player's shot is selected. From that spot, this game varies from a normal scramble in that the person whose tee shot was selected isn't eligible to play the next shot. Only three team members play a second shot. If your second shot is selected, you can't hit the third shot. This process continues until the ball is holed. A variation of this game calls for the player whose shot is selected to sit out until the ball is holed or the group hits four shots on that hole. On the fifth shot, the entire group can return to action.

STRATEGY TIPS: If two players hit good drives, don't use the better player's tee shot, as you will likely need that golfer for the important second shot. If you are playing the multiplayer elimination version, try to eliminate the weakest member of the group as soon as possible, or save that player for an easy stroke, such as a tap-in putt.

ELIMINATOR (ALSO KNOWN AS IN THE BUCKET)

Foursomes compete in a best-ball format except that, as a player's score is used for a hole, that person is eliminated from the competition, leaving only three players to supply the best ball, then two players, then one player. After everyone in the group has had one score used in the best-ball tournament, each becomes eligible again to have their score recorded as the team score.

STRATEGY TIPS: Use the weaker players' scores as quickly as possible, leaving the best player in the group as the lone player as often as possible. But if someone in the group makes a birdie, don't be tempted to take a weaker player's par on the hole.

FLORIDA SCRAMBLE

See game description under **Dropout Scramble** in this chapter.

GEIBERGER

See game description under **59** in the Side Games chapter.

GET OUT

Using the scramble format, teams are eliminated from the competition for making bogey or worse at any point during the round. At the end of the round, the remaining teams compare their 18-hole scores to determine the winner. Handicaps can be used but are not recommended, since making a bogey is difficult in a scramble, even for four mid- to high-handicappers.

STRATEGY TIPS: A group is most likely to make bogey on the par 3s, where there is little room for recovery. Focus on these holes. Not only is it important to avoid bogey, but you also should consider your overall score. Depending on the number of groups, the winning team is usually 10-under or lower.

IN THE BUCKET

See game description under **Eliminator** in this chapter.

IRISH FOUR-BALL

See game description under **1-2-3 Best Ball** in this chapter.

IRISH FOUR-BALL MODIFIED STABLEFORD

A foursome plays as a team against other foursomes using a Modified Stableford method of scoring. (One suggestion: one point for a bogey, two for a par, four for a birdie, and eight for an eagle.) There are many variations to the point totals as well as the number of players' scores that count per hole. One way to score the competition is to count only two scores per foursome per hole for the entire round. Another option: On holes 1–6, the individual team member who records the highest point total on a hole provides the team's score. On holes 7–11, the two individuals with the highest point totals provide the team's score. On holes 12–15, three players' scores are needed. On the final two holes, everybody's point total counts.

STRATEGY TIPS: Depending on the number of golfers' scores needed per hole, you should be encouraged to take risks when players in your group already have secured an acceptable number of points for that hole. In other words, if two players have made par, then going for a birdie with a firm, fast putt makes sense. So does trying to hole out from off the green rather than lagging the ball close. On holes where everyone's score counts, it's imperative that no player gets shut out, so play safe and try to make sure your team gets at least four points.

LADDER

A long-term competition played over the course of a season, a long weekend, etc. Players or teams are ordered from high to low depending on their handicap, with better players at the top of the ladder. Any player can challenge any of the three players listed above him on the ladder. If the challenger wins (typically a 9- or

18-hole match with handicap strokes allocated), this player moves into the ladder rung occupied by the loser and the loser assumes the challenger's spot. If the challenger loses, he cannot challenge another player on the ladder again until he successfully defends his position on the ladder. The only exception is the player on the bottom rung of the ladder, who can challenge at any time. On the final day or week of competition, a player is eligible to play only the person on the rung immediately above him for a final spot on the ladder. Payouts typically descend, with the top three golfers or teams usually receiving the bulk of the money.

STRATEGY TIPS: If you're going to get anywhere in this competition, you have to make challenges that are at least two steps ahead of your position. If you see a player or team ahead of you that you know you can beat, go for it.

LONE RANGER

See game description under **Money Ball** in this chapter.

MODIFIED STABLEFORD

A game where points are earned depending on a golfer's score. There are many variations to the points system, including subtracting points for double bogey or worse. However, typically the point structure is as follows: one point for bogey, two for par, four for birdie, and eight for eagle. The format can include handicap strokes, but the point structure might have to be altered accordingly. For instance, a net double bogey might be worth minus-1 point. The player with the most points at the end of the round wins and gets paid by the other players based on the difference in their point totals. The player with the second-most points is paid by the other two players, and so on.

STRATEGY TIPS: Making bogeys seems like a good thing since you are accruing points on every hole, but it's better to try to make a couple of birdies (net or gross). This will free you to play more aggressively and not worry about taking a big number on the scorecard.

MONEY BALL (ALSO KNOWN AS LONE RANGER)

A foursome plays a stroke-play competition in which each member plays either her own ball or a "money ball," which is rotated among members of the group on each hole. It can start with whichever player the group chooses. The lowest score from the group of players without the money ball on each hole is counted, as is the score of the player holding the money ball. These two scores are added together for a one-hole team score. The other two scores are thrown out. There are many variations of this game. A common option is to have teams eliminated if they actually lose the money ball in the process of playing a hole. Or if the money-ball player makes birdie, that score is doubled and the other three scores don't matter. Handicaps can be used with this game, but it's often more fun if the player with the money ball receives no strokes.

STRATEGY TIPS: The money-ball player should never take chances. Often, a bogey with the money ball is a good score. Focus on hitting fairways and avoiding trouble. Keep the ball in play, and let the rest of your team focus on making a good score to go with the money-ball score. If the money-ball player is in good shape, the team members should play aggressively to make birdies.

ONE CLUB

See game description in the Twosomes chapter.

PEORIA SYSTEM

Like the Callaway System (see definition in this chapter), this is a tournament format for players who don't have an official USGA Handicap Index. In this format, tournament organizers wait for everyone to tee off, then select six holes to be used to determine team scores. This can be done randomly, but it's a good idea to select two par 3s, two par 4s, and two par 5s. The teams will have no idea which holes are being counted until the tournament is complete. Once the holes are selected, each player's score for those six holes is totaled, then multiplied by three and subtracted from the course's par. That number becomes the player's score.

STRATEGY TIPS: Since hole selection is random, there's little a player can do except try to avoid making a big number on any hole. The fact that only six holes are being used to determine a player's score also means that having a couple of "blow-up" holes shouldn't discourage you from playing hard the rest of the round.

POWERBALL

A scramble where four holes are designated as "powerball" holes. At those holes, only one member of the foursome can tee off for the group, and that shot must be used. Each powerball tee shot has to be played by a different member of the foursome. The powerball is typically played from the forward tee. The other 14 holes are played like a normal scramble.

STRATEGY TIPS: If there's an opportunity to drive a par 4, put your longest or best player on the tee for that powerball hole. If there's a tough par 3, even from the forward tees, put your best player on that hole. Save your worst player for a par 5 since the group can still make birdie even if the tee shot is bad.

QUOTA

See game description in the Foursomes chapter.

RANSOM

See game description under **Mix and Match** in the Foursomes chapter.

SCRAMBLE

One of the most common formats for multiple-group games. Each team member hits a tee shot. The group selects one of those shots for play. From that spot, each team member hits another shot, and one of those balls is selected. This process continues until the ball is holed and the team score is recorded. Handicaps are sometimes used in conjunction with this format. Typically the total handicaps for the group are added together and divided by four, and that represents the team handicap, with strokes being allocated on those holes. For instance, a group consisting of a 2-handicap, a 4-handicap, a 6-handicap, and an 8-handicap would have a team handicap of 5. That group would get to take a stroke off their team score on the five hardest holes as ranked on the scorecard. A variation of this format, sometimes known as a Texas Scramble, mandates that a certain number of tee shots from each player in the group must be used.

STRATEGY TIPS: Selecting the correct order of play is crucial. Many teams put their best players first and last. If the first player hits a good shot, that allows the other players in the group to play aggressively. If the first three players hit bad shots, the remaining good player can save the day. In putting, the best putter often goes second or third so the putting line can be viewed by a putt from a weaker putter.

SHAMBLE

Similar to a scramble. After each golfer hits a tee shot, the group selects the best shot. Everyone in the group then plays their own ball from the spot where the selected tee shot came to rest. The lowest score counts as the team score. A popular variation of this game is to have the two lowest scores count as the team score.

STRATEGY TIPS: Off the tee, the strategy is the same as a scramble. The player who can get the ball in the fairway most of the time goes first. Doing so alleviates tons of pressure from the other players in the group.

The most-skilled player goes last because she can handle the pressure when the other players have hit bad shots. Once the tee shot is selected, play should be less aggressive than in a scramble, but players should pay attention to how their teammates are doing. If someone has a par or birdie locked up, playing more aggressively might make sense. A steady stream of pars keeps most teams in a shamble competitive.

SHOOTOUT

A predetermined number of golfers (usually nine or 18) play against one another in a sudden-death event where at least one player is eliminated per hole. The player with the highest score on each hole is eliminated until there is only one golfer remaining. If two or more players tie for the highest score on a hole, they can either be eliminated or be forced into some kind of competition (such as a chip-off) to determine who survives to the next hole. Once a player is eliminated, the rest of the group moves to the next hole. Another player is eliminated when he records the highest score on that hole. The game ends when only one player is left. There are many variations of this game, and money is typically paid out to either the winner or the top two finishers.

STRATEGY TIPS: There's no need to play risky shots early on. Play conservatively and let other players make big mistakes that force them out of the game. Birdies are a lot more important late in the game.

STRING

Each player or team is given string—either the same length or varying lengths depending on the player or team's handicap—before the round begins. In this game, using any number of formats, including stroke play or scramble, a player or team may move a ball at rest so long as the distance the ball is moved is cut from the length of string and thrown away. When a golfer or team runs out of string, every ball must be played as it lies.

STRATEGY TIPS: Before the round, ask whether a ball can be moved from its resting spot into the hole. If it can, obviously a just-missed eagle or birdie putt might prove more valuable than a tap-in for birdie or par. If it can't be used for holed putts (most of the time, it can't be used to hole putts), try to use string only when it's nearly a guarantee to save a shot or more—such as from a plugged lie in a bunker or from an awkward-stance situation.

THREE-CLUB MONTE

See game description in the Twosomes chapter.

Each member of a foursome plays his or her own ball in a stroke-play format. The low and high scores are combined to make up the team score on that hole. The two scores that are used are the low ball and the high ball. So if on a par 3 the four players score 3, 3, 4, and 6, the team score is 9 (3 + 6). The exception is if someone in the group makes a birdie or better. Then the team can combine its two low balls on that hole. Handicaps can be used in this game.

STRATEGY TIPS: Determine whether this is a net or gross scoring game. If it's net, then go for as many birdies as possible to keep the score in check. The team should play aggressively whenever one player has secured par or better. When assembling a team, all it takes is for one really bad player to make your scores ugly, so try to find players who are consistent and respectable. Two bogeys isn't a bad score. A bogey and quadruple bogey are deadly.

WHEEL

Using the best-ball format, a player selects up to three other golfers in the tournament field (a minimum field of 16 is required). These players are the golfer's partners, although they do not have to play together. At the end of their respective rounds, the player takes his scorecard and matches it up with each partner's scorecard, trying to compile the lowest best-ball score possible. That score is then compared with the partnerships made by other people in the tournament field, and the low best-ball score wins money thrown into a pot before the round. Usually the amount of money each golfer contributes to the pot is determined by the number of partners the golfer selects. The amount doubles for two partners and doubles again for three, so a player who put in $5 for one partner would put in $10 for two partners and $20 for three partners.

STRATEGY TIPS: The more partners you have selected, the better your odds of winning. However, you also are risking more money, so don't overdo it. It makes sense to choose partners who have a low handicap since they can cover you if you make a bad score on a hole. However, it might be useful to also have partners who get a lot of strokes via handicap, so try to find a nice blend of high- and low-handicap partners. It's likely that one or more of your partners in the event won't be playing with you, so it can be difficult to plan your course strategy around a partner's score. That means you should play conservatively unless there is no serious danger on a hole. Take double bogey out of play.

CHAPTER 5

SIDE GAMES

(to be played in conjunction with other games)

Sometimes one bet is just not enough. That's why hard-core golfers often add a number of side bets to their gambling games. Not only do they feel it makes the round more rewarding, it also keeps parties interested in the round long after the main bet has been decided.

3s AND 4s

At the end of the round, the player with the scorecard that has the most 3s and 4s on it wins a side pot, or the other players pay him an amount based on how many more 3s and 4s he has than the losers.

STRATEGY TIPS: Take advantage of the par 3s, and ensure that you come away with a 3 or 4 on every one of those holes.

A putting game during the round where one golfer challenges another's ability to avoid a three-putt on any hole. The golfer who challenges gets two points if the other player can't hole out in two putts or less. If the competitor does hole out in two putts or less, the challenger owes the golfer three points.

STRATEGY TIPS: Though it seems reasonable to challenge if another golfer faces a tough putt, it's a much better idea to monitor the putting success of fellow golfers and prey only on the weak. If someone is struggling, even simple two-putts can turn into three-putt nightmares—especially with a wager on the line.

59 (ALSO KNOWN AS GEIBERGER)

The first player to reach a gross score of 59 pays the other players in the group a point for every stroke they are below 59 at that moment. Or the group can decide the payout amount before the round.

STRATEGY TIPS: This game is good for groups in which the players have roughly the same ability. If that's the case, play conservatively and avoid making big numbers. Watch your score in relation to the other players. If you have a big cushion toward the back nine, it's OK to play more aggressively.

AIR PRESSES

A one-hole wager between two golfers called while a ball is airborne. A golfer can call this press—for a pre-determined wager amount—on an opponent only when the opponent's ball is in the air. The press must be accepted, and means the challenger thinks he or she will have a lower score on the hole than the opponent. The opponent can double the bet after the challenger's next shot. Then the challenger can triple the bet, and so on.

STRATEGY TIPS: A ball headed out-of-bounds is ripe for an air press. But it's also a good idea to press on a hole you play particularly well, even if your opponent hits a shot in play. Sometimes air pressing a good shot will rattle an opponent.

APPEARANCE FEES

See game description under **Honors** in this chapter.

ARNIES

Named after Arnold Palmer, who was a master at making pars despite hitting errant tee shots. Each player pays a bonus to any member of the foursome who makes par or better on a par 4 or par 5 without playing a shot from the fairway. Driving a par 4 doesn't usually qualify for an Arnie, but get this clarified before setting this side bet.

STRATEGY TIPS: No one should intentionally play to miss the fairway, but on "wide-open" holes where missing the fairway isn't that big a deal, consider this motivation to make par. It's also easy to collect an Arnie on a short par 4.

BARKIES

Each player pays a bonus to any member of the foursome who makes par or better on a hole despite hitting a tree at some point during play of the hole.

STRATEGY TIPS: If you hit a shot into the woods, try to escape on your next shot, but advance the ball far enough to have a short iron into the green. You should be able to hit the green with the next shot, leaving yourself a chance to par the hole with a good putt. On a par 5, it's OK to hit driver off the tee knowing you don't have to reach the green in two shots.

BOBS (ALSO KNOWN AS PROXES, PROXIES, OR PAR-3 GREENIES)

On a par 3, the player who hits a shot on the green in regulation and is closest to the pin is eligible for the bob (one point). That player must make par or better to secure the point. If the player doesn't make par or better, the point carries over to the next par 3, which is now worth two points.

STRATEGY TIPS: This side game is often overlooked once the regular match begins, so focus on hitting the greens on par 3s. Selecting one club longer than normal usually helps since it gives you more margin for error on hitting a good shot.

BOGEYMAN

The last player to make net bogey (or net double bogey if the group is filled with mid- to high-handicap players) during the round pays the other players a set amount, usually determined by the total number of net bogeys or double bogeys the group has made during the round so far. If each net bogey or net double bogey is worth, say, a quarter, then the last player to make that score would pay each player a quarter for every bogey made by the group.

STRATEGY TIPS: This game is all about playing well under pressure. If you aren't in possession of the bogeyman as you head into the final few holes, play safe and focus on keeping the ball in play. If you have the bogeyman, you can play as aggressively as you like down the stretch—unless one of your opponents is in trouble. If that's the case, play safe and let that player take risks to try to save net par or net bogey.

BOUNCE BACK

Anytime bad luck ("the rub of the green") causes a player to post a bad score on a hole, this golfer is entitled to redemption on the next hole by making par or better. A player who bounces back from a bad break on a previous hole with a par or better on the next hole is entitled to a point (the dollar value is decided by the group) from each member of the group.

STRATEGY TIPS: Take a deep breath and forget about the last hole. There's money on the line if you can shake off a bad break and make par. Make sure you get your tee shot into the fairway.

BUS DRIVER

There are buses leaving the station on the 1st hole and the 10th hole, and the object of this game is to *not* be driving the bus (hitting last in a group) when the bus gets to the 9th and 18th tee boxes. The last player to tee off on the final hole of each nine pays the other players in the group a set amount. Obviously, the teeing order must be maintained (no ready golf): Players with the lowest scores on the previous hole tee off first.

STRATEGY TIPS: By the time you reach the 6th or 15th holes, start positioning yourself so you're not hitting last when you get to the final hole on each nine. If you have honors, play safe. If you are hitting last, play aggressively and try to move up in the teeing order.

CLUTCH FAIRWAYS

Decide on a playing order for the three or four members in the group. A player's goal is to hit the fairway off the tee (using a driver or fairway wood is usually mandatory for club selection). Before attempting the shot, the first player on the tee puts up a certain amount (there's usually a minimum bet and a maximum bet determined before the round) and the other players have to match it. A player who hits the fairway wins the amount from each of the other three players. A player who misses pays the other players. Assuming there are 14 par 4s and par 5s (par 3s don't count), each player in the group will have three holes to earn money on. The two players who have hit the most total fairways win the right to earn money on the final two holes.

STRATEGY TIPS: When it's your turn, max out the bet only if you are sure you can hit the fairway seven or eight out of ten times you tee off on the hole. Make the minimum bet on hard holes.

DO-OVERS

A player can be made to replay any shot during the course of the round if that player prematurely complains about a shot that turns out to be OK. So if the player starts whining, per se, about a shot heading for a water hazard and it suddenly hits a tree branch and bounces into the middle of the fairway, the group can call a "do-over" and make that player hit the same shot again.

STRATEGY TIPS: Keep your mouth shut when it's your turn to play. However, keep in mind that if a good player hits a shot that turns out to be acceptable, but not good, it's not always a good idea to call a "do-over" since that player would have a good chance of improving with the next shot.

DOUBLE TROUBLE

Each player puts money into a side pot, and the player who goes the longest without making a double bogey or worse during the round wins the pot. If two players or more get through 18 holes without making a double bogey, then the last player to make a bogey on a hole, starting from number 18 and going to number 1, wins. If everyone makes a double bogey early in the round, the game can repeat.

STRATEGY TIPS: Anyone with a 15-handicap or lower has a decent chance of winning this game. Simply play smart and avoid penalty strokes. It's a great game for understanding course strategy. A par 3 is the easiest spot for making double bogey, so do whatever it takes to avoid water, including laying up if necessary.

DUKE OF HAZARDS

Any golfer who plays a shot out of a hazard and makes net par or better wins a predetermined amount. Note: Bunkers are hazards.

STRATEGY TIPS: If you can get a club on it, there's no harm in trying to advance the ball out of a water hazard to give yourself a chance at making par. Balls partially submerged in water should be treated like sand shots—open the blade of a wedge and make a full swing.

ECLECTIC

See game description under **Ringer Score** in this chapter.

FAIRWAYS

Using the skins-game format, the first player to hit a fairway off the tee when no one else in the group does wins the skin and any other skins that have been uncollected up to that point.

STRATEGY TIPS: You'd be surprised at how accurate your tee shots can become once money is on the line. The driver stays in the bag except for wide fairways. Don't be afraid to tee off with a 7-iron if that means keeping an opponent from winning a bunch of skins. Keep the ball in the fairway, and a side benefit should be an improvement in your scores—especially for high-handicappers.

FAIRWAYS AND GREENS

Can be played as a twosome, threesome, or foursome game. A player earns a point for hitting a fairway or a green when no one else does. The value of hitting a green can be doubled since it's typically harder than hitting a fairway.

STRATEGY TIPS: If you're the last player to tee off or hit onto a green, you are at a huge advantage since you know the stakes. Play your most accurate club off the tee whenever there's a chance to earn points. If someone else is already in the fairway, or multiple players are in the fairway, take out your driver and try to get into a great position to hit the green with your next shot.

FLAGS (ALSO KNOWN AS TOMBSTONE)

Each player puts money into a side pot. Then their course handicap is added to the course's par. That number represents the shots it will take the player to navigate the course. Whenever the player uses up the allotment of strokes, assuming it comes before finishing the course, that spot is marked by staking an imaginary flag. The player who travels the farthest on their stroke allotment wins the side pot. Another way to settle the bet is to have the other players pay a set amount for every hole short they finish of the winning player's flag. Players who stake their flag in the middle of a hole do not get to count the hole as being completed. So if one player stakes a flag on the second shot of the 16th hole and another player puts a flag down in the middle of the 18th, then the first player would owe the second player the value of two holes.

STRATEGY TIPS: Big numbers are killers, so avoid making double bogeys. Divide your stroke allotment by 18 to get a sense of how many strokes you can afford on each hole, and use course management to ensure you don't go over that amount. If you are six or seven shots ahead of pace, it's OK to play aggressively, but never play aggressively if you are way behind. Instead, focus on going as far as you can on the remaining shots.

GEIBERGER

See game description under **59** in this chapter.

HONEST JOHN

Players write down the score they think they will shoot that day and throw money into a pot. The person who comes closest to their predicted score wins the pot. Note: No one knows anyone else's bid until the game is over, so have each player write down a score, seal the paper, and hand it in before the round begins.

STRATEGY TIPS: If you're getting killed in the regular game but have a chance to shoot your predicted score, you might try to play to that number. But if your team is winning the big match, you need to shoot as low as you can.

HONORS (ALSO KNOWN AS APPEARANCE FEES OR TEES)

A side game for any number of players in a group. A coin flip or some other form of chance decides which player or team tees off first. If that player or team wins that hole, thus maintaining the honor (tee box), a point is awarded. If the hole is halved, the player or team continues to tee off first but is not awarded a point. If the team has honors and loses the hole, it loses three points and the honors (tee box). As long as the team has honors and continues to win holes, it gets additional points. Point values can double with each hole consecutively won or stay the same. A variation of this game allows for a team to earn one point for every hole (except the first) where it controls the tee box.

STRATEGY TIPS: Don't worry so much about losing three points for losing the tee box, since your opponent(s) also will lose three points the minute you wrestle tee box honors back from them. Focus on racking up points when you have honors.

JUNK

This employs using any combination of side bets such as barkies, sandies, Arnies, hitting fairways in regulation, getting closest to the pin on par 3s, making natural birdies, and so on. These side bets are tallied as separate achievements for each golfer and paid out by the other golfers in the group. For instance, a player who scores a sandy and a natural birdie would receive a predetermined amount from each player in the group for each achievement.

STRATEGY TIPS: If you are getting killed in a team game, concentrate on all the ways to make your money back with side bets. At worst it will get your mind off the pressure of trying to make a big comeback in a nassau. At best you'll rack up enough junk points to lessen the sting of losing the team bet. It's a good idea to make the money awarded for side bets less than the regular bet since the focus should always start on the main bet.

LOW PUTTS (ALSO KNOWN AS TOTAL PUTTS)

Simply put, the lowest number of putts needed for an entire round wins. Clarify before playing whether this includes putts from off the green or from the fringe. There can be a side-pot payout, or the player can receive a certain amount for every putt more the other players in the group needed to finish the round.

STRATEGY TIPS: If fringe putts don't count, then missing greens gives a great advantage to players who have a good short game. They can chip on close to the hole and one-putt.

MURPHY

Players who are off the green can call for a murphy and try to hole out from that spot in one or two shots. If successful, the player is paid a predetermined amount.

It's wise to decide before the round whether fringe shots are eligible for a murphy. The game can include a penalty for someone who calls for a murphy but fails to execute.

STRATEGY TIPS: If the fringe is included in the game—always check on this before the game starts—you should call murphy as often as you are on the fringe. Another good time for a murphy is when the ball is sitting short of the green on the neck and the pin is relatively close.

MUTT AND JEFF

Each player's score on all the par 3s is added up. In a separate tabulation, the same is done with each player's score on all the par 5s. The player with the low score on par 3s is paid a predetermined amount, as is the one who scored low on the par 5s. The number of strokes the winner made (compared to the other players' totals) could determine the amount, or it can be a set side-pot amount. Handicaps can be used.

STRATEGY TIPS: Playing conservatively on all the par 3s and par 5s is smart in this game, since aggressive players might birdie one of the holes but then take a big number on another.

NASTIES

Any hole-out from off the green wins a point.

STRATEGY TIPS: Decide whether fringe putts count (they usually don't). Anytime you can putt from off the green, do it, as it makes accuracy a lot easier. Don't leave up-and-down shots short.

NO PUTTS

Determine the winner by totaling all strokes used without a putter. The low number from a group wins either a point for every stroke lower than opponents' strokes or takes a side pot. Decide before the round whether the putter can be used off the green.

STRATEGY TIPS: For tap-ins on the green, consider using a club other than the putter. If putters must be used on the green, focus on hitting greens in regulation, no matter how far from the flag the ball comes to rest.

ON IN TWO

Used with any game format, each player must use the longest club in their bag (driver can be excluded) for the second shot on a par 5, no matter where the tee shot lands. A player who successfully hits a par 5 green in two gets two points from each player. If the player converts it to a birdie, two more points are added. If the player converts it to an eagle, four more points are awarded from each player.

STRATEGY TIPS: No more worrying about whether you should have gone for it on a par 5; you have to go for it. But just because you have to swing your 3-wood for your second shot doesn't mean you have to swing full. If you are in the rough, use the 3-wood to punch out and then play the hole like normal.

OUZLE FOUZLE

Players are awarded an Ouzle (Scottish term for greenie) and a predetermined amount from the other players in the group for hitting a green in regulation and then making par or better. However, they also are given a Fouzle for hitting a green in regulation and three-putting. On a par-5, hitting a green in two and three-putting for par also gets you a Fouzle. Players who make a Fouzle must pay each member of the group a predetermined amount.

STRATEGY TIPS: Big greens are fertile ground for Fouzles, and so are situations with severe downhill putts. Attack greens cautiously, leaving approach shots below the hole when possible.

PAR-3 GREENIES

See game description under **Bobs** in this chapter.

POKER

Each player tries to build the best hand possible on the front nine, and then the best hand possible on the back nine using their scores. Lower numbers trump higher numbers, so a player who makes four 3s on the front nine beats a player who makes four 4s. The hierarchy of poker hands are as follows: five of a kind, four of a kind, full house, straight, three of a kind, and two pair.

STRATEGY TIPS: The game favors a consistent player who can string together a bunch of the same scores. It has less to do with shooting a low score. In that regard, it's a good side game when the group has players with varying handicaps. Making five 3s, however, ought to win one hand almost every time.

POLEYS

Any player who sinks a putt outside the length of the flagstick is awarded a poley and receives a predetermined amount from the other players in the group. A variation of this game allows for anyone, including the player who is about to putt, to call for a poley. This can be done only if a putt is outside the length of a flag-stick. If the player sinks the putt, the other players in the group pay the winner two points. If the player two-putts, no money is exchanged. But, the player who three-putts pays each member of the group two points.

STRATEGY TIPS: Obviously, having a putt just outside the flagstick is ideal for calling a poley. But also keep in mind that some three-putts can come from short distances, particularly if the green has two tiers or if you are facing a dicey downhill putt.

POTTY MOUTH

Any player who curses during the round can choose to pay a fine to the others in the group or play the next hole with only one full-swing club and a putter.

STRATEGY TIPS: A good game to play along with skins, since having to play a hole with one club can really hamper a player's chance of winning a skin. Keep your mouth shut or invent new expletives that are rated PG.

PROGRESSIVE UP-AND-DOWNS

The first player to save par from off the green is paid a predetermined amount. That amount doubles for every subsequent up-and-down until the round ends. The group should determine before the start of the round if the fringe counts as off the green (it usually doesn't for this game).

STRATEGY TIPS: Late in the round, play for the edges of greens, giving yourself a chance at an easy up-and-down with a putt from the rough, etc.

PROXES

See game description under **Bobs** in this chapter.

PUTT FOR DOUGH

Every one-putt is worth a point value depending on the distance of the putt. The group can decide the breakdown. Once everyone is on the green, the member of the foursome who is farthest from the cup gets four points for one-putting the hole. The next player gets three points for a one-putt, the next player gets two points, and the closest to the hole gets one point for a one-putt. Anyone who three-putts loses a point, and anyone who holes out from off the green earns five points. Players are paid for each point they have amassed.

STRATEGY TIPS: Putting from off the green is a great

way to earn a five-pointer. But the player who misses a lot of greens and can chip it close is always in great shape to earn points. You can really sharpen your short game and putting skills with this side bet, but you have to get the putt to the hole.

RINGER SCORE (ALSO KNOWN AS ECLECTIC OR SELECTED SCORE)

Great for golf trips or multiround tournaments. At the end of the trip or competition, each golfer examines all of their scorecards and selects the lowest number they made on each hole (either from the same course or numerically, such as all the first holes at every course played). The low scores are tallied, producing an 18-hole score to be matched against those of other players.

STRATEGY TIPS: During the trip or tournament, remembering where you had really bad holes is imperative. Try to replace all double bogeys or worse with bogeys or better by the end of the competition. That means, don't take unnecessary risks.

SANDIES AND SUPER OR EXOTIC SANDIES

A sandy is awarded to any player who gets up-and-down from a greenside bunker for par or better. It can also be awarded—depending on what your group decides— from a fairway bunker. A super or exotic sandy can be awarded to any player who makes par or better despite being in a fairway bunker and a greenside bunker on the same hole. This usually pays double the amount of a regular sandy.

STRATEGY TIPS: Sandies are rare in handicap play, so the amount awarded should be significant, but still far less than the bet for the main game being played in conjunction. Don't be afraid of bunkers on par 5s, as the extra shot often makes it easy to make par. Give yourself as many chances as you can to putt for sandies by focusing on getting the ball anywhere on a green.

SCRUFFY

Any player who hits a tee shot that lands off the fairway or green can call a scruffy, meaning the player thinks he or she will make a par or better (gross) on that hole. If the player succeeds, the other players each pay the scruffy winner a predetermined amount. However, a player who fails must then pay each of the other players a set amount. A variation of this game allows the other players to refuse or double the bet. Another variation specifies that the ball must be in a bunker, hazard, deep rough, or woods to be eligible for a scruffy.

STRATEGY TIPS: Depending on the style of game you

are playing, shots just off the fairway on a par 4 or just off the green on a par 3 are great opportunities to call a scruffy. Par 5s are even better, as most players can get back in the fairway and advance the ball significantly, even if the tee shot lands in the woods.

SELECTED SCORE

See game description under **Ringer Score** in this chapter.

SNAKE

The player who three-putts last in the round pays the other members of the group, with the amount typically determined by the number of three-putts the group has accumulated. If each three-putt is worth 50 cents, for example, the player who makes the group's 10th and final three-putt pays the others $5 each. Progressive snake can also be played so the amount of the bet doubles every time another group member three-putts. On the final green, the hole must be played out in order of farthest away. One variation holds that a four-putt on the final hole overrides the last three-putt. The player with the four-putt gets the snake. In an effort to speed up play, obvious tap-ins can be conceded as holed putts until the group reaches, say, the final four or five holes. Then everything must be putted out.

STRATEGY TIPS: If you don't have the snake, hitting the 18th green in regulation, unless the ball is close to the flag, has a real potential for danger. Be leery of big greens. A smart play might be to lay up just short of the green and try to get up-and-down. Better yet, play to the back fringe. The first putt on the last hole is crucial. This is a great game to improve your putting and your ability to deal with pressure.

STEALIES

If you're playing greenies (aka closest to the pin), a stealie goes to someone who makes birdie when they aren't closest to the pin in regulation. Essentially, the player steals the hole from the player who had the greenie and nullifies it. The bet usually pays double the original closest-to-the-pin bet.

STRATEGY TIPS: Mid- to high-handicap groups rarely make more than one birdie per round, but a par 5 is always a great opportunity for a stealie because lots of players can be on the green in regulation.

SUPER GREENIES

Points are awarded for hitting greens in regulation, but the number of points depends on the distance away from the green the player's shot started. For 200-yard and longer shots, nine points are awarded. Then for every 30-yard increment less than 200, the point value drops by two, so a 199-yard to 170-yard shot is seven points, a 169- to 140-yard shot is five points, a 139- to 110-yard shot is three points, and a 109- to 80-yard shot is one point. Point values and distance requirements can be altered. A variation of the game subtracts a point for missed greens from inside 80 yards.

STRATEGY TIPS: Focus on hitting shots to the fat part of the green, even if the pin is tucked.

TEE TO GREEN

See game description in the Twosomes chapter.

TEES

See game description under **Honors** in this chapter.

THREE-PUTT POKER

At the beginning of the round, each player antes a certain amount into a pot (say $5) and is dealt one playing card. Any player who three-putts a hole on the front nine adds to the pot (usually $1). The only way to get an additional playing card is to one-putt a hole. Usually, using the putter from anywhere—not just on the green—counts as the first putt. After nine holes, the player with the best five-card hand wins the pot, and the game starts over on the back nine.

STRATEGY TIPS: Determine before the round if there is a limit to the number of cards a player can be dealt. Obviously, you could end up with 10 cards if you one-putt every hole on a given nine. If you miss a green, focus on chipping close to the hole to make a one-putt tap-in an easy way to pick up a fresh card.

TOMBSTONE

See game description under **Flags** in this chapter.

TRIFECTA

A good side bet for mid- to high-handicappers, any player in a group who pars three holes in a row is said to have made a trifecta and is paid a predetermined amount by the other players. If the player then continues the run with a fourth or fifth consecutive par, there can be a bonus amount added. To enhance the game, handicaps should be used only for players with indexes higher than, say, nine.

STRATEGY TIPS: You need to pay attention to this game only if you've made two pars in a row. On the third hole, play smart and give yourself a chance at a decent par putt. In other words, find the fairway with any club off the tee and leave your second shot in a place where you can either two-putt or get up-and-down for par.

TROUBLE

See game description in the Foursomes chapter.

WIZ, SHEIKH, DUCK, LUMBERJACK

The last player to hit a bad shot in one of these four categories in a round pays the rest of the group a set amount. The Wiz is the last player to hit a shot out of bounds. The Sheikh is the last player to hit a ball in a bunker. The Duck is the last player to hit a ball in the water. And the Lumberjack is the last player to hit a tree.

STRATEGY TIPS: You really don't have to start paying attention to this until about the 13th hole. But from there on, do your best to avoid at least three of the four. Figure that even if you lose one of these bets, you will get paid from another player for the other three and end up making money.

CHAPTER 6

OTHER GAMES

For golfers who have time to kill between rounds—or who are waiting for the group in front of them to clear during a round—there's nothing like making a little side bet unrelated to the actual round. These games give you something to do when there's nothing else to do.

AROUND THE WORLD

On the practice putting green, a golfer places five to seven balls around a hole at various distances and has to sink them all in the fewest amount of strokes. An opponent attempts to beat that number. The player who finishes with a higher stroke count must pay for every extra putt needed to hole out all the balls.

STRATEGY TIPS: A three-putt in this game is a killer, but so is not making a few one-putts. Don't worry about lagging. Be especially aggressive on uphill putts.

BURN THE EDGE

Played on the practice putting green. The object is to hit a putt that hits the rim of the cup but doesn't fall into the hole. The determining factor for whether it burned the edge is if the ball changes direction. The first player to burn the edge of five different holes wins.

STRATEGY TIPS: Honing a stroke that misses the hole might seem counterproductive, but what you are doing is narrowing your focus to a precise target. It can make you a better putter. The trick is to be aggressive and get the ball rolling at a speed where hitting the edge will throw it off line. A slower putt might tumble in if it catches the edge.

CROSS COUNTRY

Can be played anywhere except an active golf course. The game is simple. Pick a starting point and a destination. The player who reaches the destination in the fewest strokes wins. Play order is determined by who is farthest from the hole.

STRATEGY TIPS: Remember that playing the holes in order isn't necessarily the best way to reach the destination in the fewest number of strokes. If you can hit shots across fairways and over obstacles, take the most direct route.

CUTTHROAT

While waiting on a tee box, each member of a group places a ball on the ground next to one of the tee markers. Using a driver, each player tries to hit a ball so it strikes the tee marker on the opposite side of the box. Then, once that marker has been hit, the player tries to hit the marker where the game began. The first player to do it wins. The order of play alternates, but a player who hits the tee marker gets to go again immediately. If a player misses the marker, it's the next player's turn.

STRATEGY TIPS: Hitting the tee marker is important, but so is knocking another player's ball out of an ideal position. It's wise to try to stymie an opponent by blocking his or her line to the tee marker.

HORSE

On the practice putting green, a player tries to sink a putt. If it is holed, the other players in the game have to sink the same putt or they receive the letter "H." (If it's a miss, the next player in line gets to try to make a putt of their choice.) The player who sank the original putt then gets to hit another putt. If it goes in, the opponents have to make it or they get saddled with "O." This continues until a player has been given the letters H-O-R-S-E, at which time that player is eliminated from the game. The last player left wins and can collect the pot.

STRATEGY TIPS: When you lead off, try to make simple three- and four-foot putts with a little break. The short length of the putt will increase the odds of making it and getting another turn. If you do make it, your opponents are going to know they have to match the putt or receive another letter. The extra pressure will make a difference in how they putt. Save the 10- to 15-footers for when you have a player down to the last letter.

HURDLES

A chipping game where the object is to get your ball the closest to a target from a certain distance, so long as the ball carries over an obstacle. On a tee box, for instance, a chip from one tee marker might have to fly over a club on the ground before rolling to the other tee marker. You get one point for clearing the hurdle and another for being closest to the pin. You lose a point for not clearing the hurdle. The first player to five points wins.

STRATEGY TIPS: Use a lower-lofted wedge or 9-iron to hit a low-trajectory shot. These clubs don't have the bulging bounce (bottom edge of the clubhead) of a sand or lob wedge, so it's easy to make crisp contact with the ball despite a thin lie on tee-box turf.

MARKER MATCH

Each player throws money into a pot. Playing in order from farthest away from the hole (who plays first is determined by lot), each player chips from a spot on the tee box to a tee marker. After striking the tee marker, each player tries to hit the opposite tee marker to win the game. Any player who hits the first marker from the starting point gets to hit their next shot immediately. Otherwise, the game is played in order.

STRATEGY TIPS: Allow for less roll on the slower surface of a tee box, but play a lower-lofted wedge for accuracy.

PULL BACK

A game for two to four players. A three-hole putting course is decided and the object is to hole out in the fewest strokes. A player who makes a putt can then choose to make another stroke or pull another player's ball back two club-lengths from where it lies.

STRATEGY TIPS: If an opponent has a three-footer or less for a next shot, it's a good idea to move them back the six feet or so that two club-lengths will provide. Otherwise, if you hole a putt, your best option is to putt again.

RANGE ROVER

Five targets are selected on a driving range. The targets can be as precise as a pole or flagstick or as broad as a fence or green and should vary in length and direction from the tee. Players alternate hitting shots, and the first one to hit all five targets wins.

STRATEGY TIPS: Going for the hardest targets first sets up a fast and furious finish, so don't worry if you fall behind. Also, focus on hitting low-trajectory shots, as they are much easier to control in terms of accuracy.

SEVEN POINT (ALSO KNOWN AS SEVEN UP)

On the practice putting green, each player puts money into a pot and then tries to amass seven points. The order of play can be chosen by lot and each player gets to putt after the first player has chosen a particular putt for the group. On the next hole, another player gets to choose unless someone one-putts the first hole. In that case the one-putt player gets to choose. A golfer gets two points for a one-putt if no one else one-putts. If there's a tie, no one gets points. A golfer gets one point for having the closest putt to the hole when no one sinks the putt. Any player who three-putts, regardless of whether someone already has, gets minus-three points.

STRATEGY TIPS: Obviously, you never want to three-putt, so focus on making good lag putts that have a chance to die into the hole.

THROUGH THE BAG

A driving-range game where three targets are selected: short, medium, and long. The object of the game is to hit each target with at least three but no more than four different clubs. Once a target is hit, the club is taken out of the bag and put off to the side. The first player to get through all the clubs in the bag wins a predetermined amount. Sometimes there can be a set amount for every club the other player still has in the bag. Players alternate hitting shots, and it doesn't matter how a ball strikes a target. For fun, the putter can be part of the game, but usually isn't.

STRATEGY TIPS: What are your strengths? If you are straight off the tee, go for the farthest target first. Another tactic is to use your harder-to-hit clubs for the medium and short targets if you can reach the longest target with a club that's easier to control.

CHAPTER 7

STRATEGY

You've got the tee time, you've got the foursome, and you've got 10 minutes before you're on the first tee box. So now what? Understanding what to play, how to play, and for how much can be the difference between having a glorious Saturday morning and one in which you have to raid your savings account to pay your debt (and hope your spouse doesn't see the bank statement).

Start by deciding on the right game. If you're the kind of person who says "I don't care" when the subject is broached, don't be surprised when you're reaching into your wallet at the end of the round. Deciding on the right game is a huge aspect of golf gambling. Obviously, the number of players involved will eliminate a lot of potential games.

But there's more to it than that. Are you the kind of person who likes to keep it simple? If so, a nassau or closeout or best ball is the way to go. If you like something more intricate, perhaps Las Vegas or the Points Game makes sense. Also, consider the right game for the other members of your group. If they are your friends, and no one wants anyone else in the group sulking on the way home, then choose a game that is simple, fun, and that can produce an unpredictable outcome such as Sixes, Strike Three, or Trifecta. If it's a group of strangers and you're looking to make money, choose a game that you know well—especially if it's one your opponents don't know very well.

Once you have your main game settled, decide whether side bets (often known as junk or garbage) will be included in the round. Again, agree only to side bets that favor your abilities on the golf course. If you spray the ball off the tee, then playing Fairways isn't a good idea. If you're a good putter, then Snake might be right for you. Avoid accepting a bet that has too many side bets. Some garbage actually rewards bad play. For instance, barkies are awarded to players who make par or better after hitting any tree on the hole. These bets are counterproductive to your goals in the main game.

In games for partners, the most important thing to remember is: If given a choice, always pick the best player available. Players with high handicaps or who are inconsistent can be a nightmare. The best player usually has the lowest handicap, but not always. If the very best player isn't available, find the guy or gal who goes low regularly or who shoots roughly the same decent round every time and you've just dramatically increased your chances of winning. This player will have a fair share of good holes and take some of the pressure off you. (See "ham and egg" in Golf Gambler's Vocabulary.) High-handicappers might seem alluring when they are getting two shots on a short par 5, but they didn't get that 26-handicap by accident. High-handicappers are as likely to take a quadruple bogey on that hole as they are to take a bogey (net birdie).

So what if the best golfer or the most consistent golfer is not available? Consider pairing with the golfer who knows the course the best. If you're the guest of a club member, then having that member as a partner will be a huge advantage. You'll be able to watch someone play the course the way it was intended to be played, and you'll have all the inside info you need on putts that break right when they should break left and holes that play a club longer or shorter than the given yardage.

What if you can't get the guy or gal who has local knowledge, and the best player in the group has already been taken? Your next best bet is to find someone you really get along with. Two players who are friends can often feed off each other. You'll find yourself playing harder and focusing more so you don't let your friend down. It's a foxhole mentality. If none of these choices are available and it seems clear you are getting stuck with a weak partner, then the best you can hope for is to barter in the game's setup for more strokes. If the game was set up to be equitable, players who complain about the team they have been given will often receive some form of extra compensation just to keep them from complaining. Go ahead. Whine and moan a little, and see if it results in getting an extra shot or two. At worst, if it's a regular group, you've already set the foundation for getting a better partner next time the gang gets together.

To recap, choose a partner in this order of importance: (1) best player available, (2) most consistent player available, (3) player with the most local knowledge, (4) a good friend.

Once the sides, game, and side bets have been chosen, the next important step is to cover all the ground rules. This is one case where reading the fine print can save you money. For instance, if you are playing a nassau, it's always a good idea to ask if presses are automatic—such as when a team or player goes two down—or are voluntary. And while you're on the subject, it's also good to know if presses can be refused and what happens at the end of the round if there is a tie. Does the bet go unsettled or is there a match of cards or do you play extra holes to determine a winner?

You need to know before the game begins if strict rules of golf are in play or if things such as rolling the ball in the fairway and gimme putts are permissible. *Golf Digest,* in its annual tournament among editors, employs a "leaf rule" for tournaments that take place in the New England autumn. If a player and opponent are reasonably sure a ball was lost under a pile of leaves, that player is allowed to drop, without penalty, as close as possible to the spot where the ball was lost, but no closer to the hole. The catch is that the player isn't eligible to win the hole, no matter what the score. The player can only halve the hole.

Things like this are good to know before play begins and will lead to fewer arguments. It's also a great idea to carry *The Rules of Golf* in your bag. Some of the simplest decisions can cross up golfers. Is a tin can found in a hazard a loose impediment or a movable obstruction? (Answer: a movable obstruction.) If you can't find the applicable rule, you should play two balls on a hole in question, note the score for each, and then let the local golf pro make the rules decision when the group returns to the clubhouse.

It's also very important to decide who keeps track of the money, the scorecard, and so on. You can insist that all bets be settled before the group leaves the course. It's wise to let your opponents keep score, because you've got better things to do, like worry about your game. Figuring out who is up or down or how much money you've won or lost is a distraction you don't need. If you're ever unsure about the status of the match, ask as often as you like. In fact, it's a decent piece of gamesmanship (see below) to continue checking on the match and score. It might annoy your opponent(s) enough for them to throw away a shot or two out of frustration.

So now you've decided on a game, a partner, who is going to keep score, and what the ground rules are. The only thing left to decide is how much to bet. Two of the 10 Commandments of Golf Gambling are (1) Never bet more money than you are comfortable losing, and (2) Always try to raise the stakes to the point that it makes your opponent(s) uncomfortable.

Money can be a huge distraction on the golf course, so it's good to know the right amount to bet. Some of the best hustlers will tell you it's the amount of the bet, and not the bet itself, that determines who wins and who loses. If you normally play $1 skins and you find yourself in a game for $20 skins, you might be more worried about the cash you could win or lose than the three foot putt you will make or miss.

Conversely, never bet an amount so low that neither you nor your opponent cares who wins. The element of risk is an important factor in gambling and will motivate you to play hard even when you aren't playing your best.

Also note the value of "junk," or side bets. The value of the side bet should be minimal compared to the main game. If you're playing $2 skins, then a side bet that rewards a player for making a gross birdie should never be more than the value of one skin. It is OK, however, for one player to make more money in side bets than in the main game since there should never be a limit on exceptional play. And if someone is getting up-and-down from the sand, dropping in birdies, and avoiding the snake, chances are that player will also be the big winner in the main game.

Once the games begin, it's time to turn your attention to the most important thing: your golf. Understanding the tendencies of your game, your partner's game, and your opponents' games can be a huge difference in making or losing money. Some golfers prefer to play hard and not worry about game strategy. Although that's not necessarily a bad thing, in truth it might not net you the greater cash reward you'll receive by understanding when to press, how to make extra cash on side bets, and where each player is getting handicap strokes.

Knowing who and where players are getting strokes is a big deal. The general rule to handicap strokes is somewhat counterintuitive to a gambler's mentality. If you are getting a stroke on a par 5, for instance, you might think of going for the green in two since you've got an extra stroke coming off your score. However, the smart play is to be conservative on a stroke hole: Lay up on that par 5, make an easy two-putt par, and you'll be rewarded with a net birdie—which almost always wins something when amateurs gambler.

Some golfers advise that you should not pay much attention to handicap strokes given or received because they can, like the size of a bet, take your attention away from the shot you are about to hit. Remember this: If it's a stroke hole, don't play too aggressively, and don't get bogged down in thoughts that distract you from making a good swing.

OK, so you're well into the match and your side is down. Is this a good time to press? Depends. If your team isn't playing well and is showing no sign of improvement, you're better off taking the standard loss rather than trying to push a bad position. Don't press. If, however, you are about to play a hole or group of holes that favors your team's strengths—such as length off the tee or natural shot shape—then by all means press away.

If you or your partner is getting a stroke on a hole and your opponent is not, a press almost always makes sense, as your odds of success have increased dramatically before the shot is hit. Pressing on the last hole of a front or back nine is a good way to make up for eight bad holes with one good one—especially if someone in your group is getting a shot. The group that is leading might be in the process of losing momentum.

Gio Valiente, a sports psychologist who helps many

professional golfers cope with on-course stress, says there are three things you can do to deal with the nervousness associated with golf betting.

"The body has a rhythm. It goes through hormonal changes constantly," he says. "And one of the things affected by this is the amount of blood flow in your hands. Since you need 'feel' to play golf well, you need good blood flow to perform the physical tasks of hitting shots, etc. If you saw Chris DiMarco playing a match in the Presidents Cup in 2005, in between holes he was squeezing a golf ball to get his blood flow going. It helped him overcome the feeling of nervousness.

"The second tip would be to perform the same routine every time you prepare to swing. Routine acts as a buffer between those bad feelings and you. It reminds you that you've done this before countless times and this shot is no more important or scary than the last.

"Finally, I would also suggest—even in match play—don't play your opponent, play the golf course. If you play your opponent, then your confidence will fluctuate with how they are playing. You just turned your confidence over to them. Play the course and worry only about the things you can control, and you can avoid being overcome when a bet is on the line."

Gamesmanship is a controversial subject when it comes to gambling and golf. For the uneducated, gamesmanship simply means anything (sportsmanlike or not) done to distract an opponent. Most purists will tell you it's a part of the game, although it should be done as deftly as possible. A few examples of subtle tactics: playing at a faster or slower pace than your opponent is accustomed to; standing quietly but just in the periphery of your opponent's vision when it's this player's time to hit a shot; and giving opponents short "gimme" putts for several holes and then making them putt out when the match gets closer to conclusion.

Others will tell you that, as long as it's within the rules, anything goes in terms of gamesmaship—there is money on the line, after all. Legendary Spanish pro Seve Ballesteros was a master of gamesmanship, and it led to his stellar 20-12-5 record in Ryder Cup play. His strategy was to get his opponent angry enough to make bad decisions on the course.

Not that Seve necessarily did these things, but some golfers have been known to jingle change in their pockets while an opponent is getting ready to putt, or point out that there are out-of-bounds markers on the right, just before an opponent tees off. Are moves like these classless? Yes. But when money is on the line, be warned that your opponent just might try a few of these things.

There are many ways to get inside a golfer's head; even paying an opponent a compliment can be distracting. Such as saying just before a player tees off, "I can't remember the last time you missed a fairway. You are really hitting it great today." Something like that can lodge a thought into an opponent's head and make them worry about impressing you with a good tee shot instead of hitting the fairway. Pressure is golf's cancer.

"The reason gamesmanship works is because some golfers have mastery orientation and others have ego orientation," Valiente says. "The ego player gets caught up in seeking validation from others, including his or her opponent. The mastery player is playing against himself and the course. Tiger Woods was once about to play a match, and his opponent told the press he thought he had a good chance of beating Tiger. When Tiger was told about it, he said, "Well, then I'm already one up. He's playing me and I'm playing the course." Gamesmanship can affect you only if you are worried about what others think or what they are doing.

It's unfortunate, but the final thing to be aware of when you're gambling is that, when money is on the line, some golfers will resort to anything to get an edge, including cheating. How do you deal with it? First, don't go looking for it. If something doesn't seem right about a player's score, or how they played a particular hole, or even an unusually high handicap, it's OK to double check, or even ask for proof if possible, but don't do it in an accusatory way. Just say something like, "I just want to make sure I've got this right. Can you tell me your score again for the fourth hole?" A player who did cheat will get the hint that you think something is wrong, and that will likely stop it from happening again.

If your opponent admits to cheating, the bet is obviously nullified (although the right thing for your opponent to do would be to declare you the winner and pay up). It would be wise never to wager with that person or team again. It should be noted, however, that you shouldn't confuse cheating with the shrewdness with which a golf bet is made. In other words, if you agree to a bet that, once the round begins, is clearly unfair, this does not make the person who offered the bet "a cheater." In this case you should swallow your pride after being duped, pay the bet, and think twice the next time this person proposes a wager. Remember, most bets are won or lost before the first ball is struck.

NASSAU (BEST BALL)

The dot indicates that Joe won a piece of junk, in this case, he got up-and-down for a sandy.

S is for snake since Ron 3-putted this hole.

HOLE	1	2	3	4	5	6	7	8	9	OUT
Blue Tees	400	398	204	421	388	164	531	360	410	3276
White Tees	392	388	190	111	365	137	520	338	400	3141
Red Tees	376	353	175	392	340	125	483	315	390	2949
Handicap	11	9	13	①	7	17	3	15	5	
Ron ₉	6	4	4	5	5	3	5	6 ⑤	4	42
Joe ₁₀	4 ⊙	4	4	7 ⁵	4	3 ᴮ	5	5	5	41
Par	4	4	3	4	4	3	5	4	4	35
+/-	+1		E					-1	(-1)	
Steve ₁₀	5	4	4	5	4	3	5	6	5	41
Herb ₁₁	6	5	3 ⑧	5	5	5	6	4	4	43

Each player's course handicap. Since Ron is a 9, Steve gets a stroke on the No. 1 handicap, and Joe and Herb get a stroke on the No. 1 and No. 2 handicap holes.

Joe's 4 means his team went 1-up in the match.

B is for a bob, or a proxy, on a par 3. Herb was closest to the pin and made par.

Negative numbers mean that the team keeping score is losing part of the match.

154

Ron and Joe were down so they pressed the remaining holes.

HOLE	10	11	12	13	14	15	16	17	18	IN	TOTAL
Blue Tees	399	415	213	409	407	545	378	176	439	3381	6657
White Tees	385	396	195	388	364	527	363	154	410	3182	6323
Red Tees	373	355	183	372	354	511	342	141	400	3031	5980
Handi-cap	12	16	14	②	6	10	4	18	8		
Ron	4	4	3	6	5	5	4 ·	4	4	39	81
Joe	5	4	3ᵖ	5	4	7ˢ	4	3	5	40	81
Par	4	4	3	4	4 Press	5	4	3	4	35	70
+/-	-1/E	-2/-1		-3/-2			⊘-3⊘	1/+1	⊟-1⊟/⊕		
Steve	6ˢ	4	3	4	4	6	5	5	4	41	82
Herb	4	③	5	③	4	5	4	6	6ˢ	40	83

Circled numbers mean the player birdied.

The circled score means this part of the match is over. Steve and Herb won 3-up.

155

SKINS

Since the first hole was halved, Ron won two skins for having the lowest score on the second hole.

Herb gets a piece of junk for his sandy.

HOLE	1	2	3	4	5	6	7	8	9	OUT
Blue Tees	430	398	205	517	478	408	533	210	460	3650
White Tees	429	354	158	461	423	386	502	191	385	3289
Red Tees	426	346	128	438	401	376	489	152	293	3049
Handicap	8	16	18	2	4	10	6	14	12	
Ron	5	4 :	4	7	4	5	5	3	5	42
Herb	6	5	3	5 :	5	6	6	3 ˢ	5	44
Par	4	4	3	5	4	4	5	3	4	36
+/-										
Travis	5	7	3	5	4	4	6	3	4	41
Dave	6	5	3	5	③ᴮ	4	6	3	4	39

Each player's course handicap.

Herb's par wins two skins since his course handicap gave him a net 4 on that hole.

Dave's birdie won a side bet known as junk. He did not win the skin, however, as Ron's par was a net 3.

156

HOLE	10	11	12	13	14	15	16	17	18	IN	TOTAL	NET SCORES
Blue Tees	492	435	499	554	161	478	479	207	411	3716	7366	
White Tees	434	421	432	480	152	430	457	195	394	3395	6684	
Red Tees	377	412	403	472	139	417	431	178	345	3174	6223	
Handi-cap	9	11	7	3	17	1	5	13	15			
Ron	5	4	6	6	4	4 ˙	6	3	5	43	85	3
Herb	5	5	6	6	3	5	6	4	4	44	88	2
Par	4	4	4	5	3	4	4	3	4	35	71	
+/-												
Travis	5	4	③ᵇ	6	4	4	5	3	4	38	79	8
Dave	6	5	4	6	②ᵇ	4	5	3	4	39	78	2

Travis wins eight skins and a piece of junk for a birdie.

Dave wins two skins and a piece of junk for a birdie.

Number of skins each player won. Three of the 18 were left on the table because the last three holes were halved.

Ron Kaspriske has been an editor at *Golf Digest* for six years and has been writing about golf for over a decade. He also coauthored a travel book called *Golf Weekends*, and writes articles for *Golf Digest* with David Leadbetter, Rick Smith, David Toms, and Chris DiMarco. The author lives in Norwalk, Conn., and usually plays $5 nassaus with junk and snake on the side.